SEVERED
YET WHOLE

March 2012

Dear Anne —

Hope you enjoy this story
based on true events — of
courage, love and faith —

Betty R

What People are Saying

It requires great courage to face and deal successfully with life's shattering blows to one's physical being. This is the absorbing story of a man who faced a loss that had been a possibility since his youth. Fortunately for him, he was married to a woman who shared his painful journey every step of the way. Their trust in God's limitless love for His children has encouraged them to live lives of blessing and inspiration that have been a positive witness to all who know them, of whom I am one.

> The Reverend Dr. Omar N. Barth
> Vero Beach, Florida

What a powerful book! Although reading, I felt like I was watching a "Hallmark movie." A masterful use of words and emotions. You will be blessed by this compelling story.

> James E. Rasa
> Author of *Dawn of the Innocent*
> and *A Dim Bulb Still Has Light*
> Georgetown, Delaware

This is an incredible story of love and faith. Over the years, I have witnessed the return of many injured GI's and followed their remarkable physical and emotional recoveries. The story that unfolds in these pages provides encouragement and direction for those facing all types of life's challenges, in or out of the military. I certainly had no idea what Stephen had to endure during his recovery. He did a remarkable job of taking care of our Rotary region's international Group Study Exchange visitors in spite of his challenges. This is a beautiful story—well written and hard to put down.

> Colonel Richard B. Harper, Jr., USAF (Ret.)
> Past President Georgetown-Millsboro Rotary Club
> Dover, Delaware

Severed Yet Whole proclaims that the Creator of the Universe has a plan for our lives. Even when we don't have the answers or understand our challenges, trusting Him is the only way to go. An important read for all, this novel is great medicine for heart and soul!

> Joyce A. Sessoms, M.Ed.
> Author of *SuccessAbility! Taking the Burden*
> *out of Navigating High School*
> Laurel, Delaware

This book offers an engaging story of hope, faith and family. It inspired me to look at life with a renewed appreciation for all I have, and it moved me emotionally to think about how I handle adversity.

Kevin Gilmore
Executive Director, Sussex County Habitat for Humanity
Georgetown, Delaware

I have personally followed Stephen and Bett on their journey of incredible challenges. Their solid commitment to God and each other is an inspiration. Absolutely, a must read.

L. Claire Smith
Author of *Choose to be Chosen*
Denton, Maryland

As the Kasperskis' pastor, I witnessed the faith, courage, and love that directed them through those uncertain and painful days. Be warned, when you enter these pages you will be entering a world defined by possibilities rather than limits and your life may never be quite the same.

The Reverend Michael Williams
Georgetown, Delaware

I was immediately drawn into this story with its roller coaster of emotions and the ever mounting challenges for all involved. Pick it up, you won't be able to put it down.

Ruth Briggs King
State Representative 37th District
Georgetown, Delaware

Perserverance, faith, and courage highlight this incredible couple's journey confronting challenge after challenge. Their never-ending love and respect for one another captivate and inspire the reader.

Bruce Zipf
President & CEO, NRT LLC (National Realty Trust LLC)
Parsippany, New Jersey

A heartwarming story! Severed Yet Whole will inspire and give hope to those who have suffered the unexpected and unwanted diagnosis, or the suddenly intrusive awareness that life will never be the same.

Dr. Bonnie Sue Lewis
Associate Professor of Mission and Native American Christianity
University of Dubuque Theological Seminary
Dubuque, Iowa

My middle school and high school students with special needs were encouraged when Stephen shared his life-changing story. Bett is a Proverbs 31 woman: trusted by her husband, dedicated to her family, quietly expressing wisdom, and worth more than rubies. As a team they are a testimony to the sustaining power of prayer and commitment. An absolute must read for you and your tweens and teens!

Mimi Blackwelder
Administrator
Destiny Christian School
Millsboro, Delaware

Uplifting from beginning to end! Angelic visitors, humor, and a supportive family and friends sustain Stephen throughout his ordeal. A gripping story that encourages us to constantly seek God's positive plan for our lives.

Karen H. Whiting
Author and speaker
Grasonville, Maryland

These pages contain "lessons for life," teaching us that true love is a selfless adventure, and true faith is a gift we humbly receive. This story is inspirational, devotional, and instructive for any who are facing challenges that threaten to overwhelm them.

The Reverend James L. Moseley
Executive Presbyter, New Castle Presbytery
Newark, Delaware

Severed
Yet Whole

A Novel

Betty Lewis Kasperski

Severed Yet Whole

Copyright © 2012 Betty Lewis Kasperski
ISBN 978-1-886068-55-1
Library of Congress Control Number: 2011945630
Personal Growth • Faith • Self-Help

Published by Fruitbearer Publishing, LLC
P.O. Box 777, Georgetown, DE 19947
302.856.6649 • FAX 302.856.7742
www.fruitbearer.com • info@fruitbearer.com
Edited by Fran D. Lowe
Cover design by Ana Tourian
Graphic design by Candy Abbott

www.SeveredYetWhole.com

The names of the two main characters, Bett and Stephen Kasperski, are real. All other names have been changed.

Unless otherwise noted, Scripture is taken from The New King James Version (NKJV), copyright © 1982 by Thomas Nelson, Inc. Used by permission. All rights reserved.

Printed in the United States of America

Dedicated

to
Stephen,
my husband
and best friend

Foreword

Those who go through hard times will find great comfort and help in this book by Betty Lewis Kasperski. I recommend this book for those who are encountering ordeals. Betty gives us a demonstration of what faith can accomplish in difficult days. It's a moving story. Read it—you will be blessed.

Tony Campolo, Ph.D.
Professor Emeritus, Eastern University
St. Davids, Pennsylvania

The Reverend Dr. Campolo is a nationally known inspirational speaker and author of thirty-six best selling books.

Prologue

The doctor entered the consultation room and closed the door. Mom grasped my hand as she had many times over the past two years and gave me her best reassuring smile. Only eleven years old—and already I was a veteran of doctor's meetings and hospital routine.

Healthier times flashed through my mind. At nine years old, my skill at "stick ball" enabled me to be the neighborhood's "first pick" when teams were chosen. I smashed that little pink ball so hard it would hit the brick warehouse wall two buildings away. And could I run! Even though I was one of the shorter boys, I ran like lightning!

Those fun-filled afternoon games halted when a sharp pain in my left thigh refused to go away. My mom's first possible medical theories for my discomfort were either muscle strain or severe dehydration-producing cramps. Her suggestion? Just rest. However, rest did not erase the problem. The pain stayed and got worse. School and sports were replaced with hospital stays and painful tests.

I used to enjoy observing the Statue of Liberty and the New York skyline from our third-floor apartment window in Jersey

City. Now the view only reminded me of medical events. I had "graduated" from doctor's office visits, to New Jersey hospitals, and now to a top New York City hospital that specialized in cancer treatment.

Positioned in front of me on Dr. Colson's desk was my ten-inch-high file, full of reports and x-rays. We waited for the final opinion.

"Good morning, you two. How are you feeling today, Stephen? Getting around okay?" Dr. Colson asked.

"I'm pretty fast on these crutches. Look how big my shoulders are. Maybe I can go out for wrestling or weight lifting at school," I said.

Mom smiled at me.

Dr. Colson looked down, not meeting my eyes. "My team has reviewed all of your tests." He looked up. "You've been a strong trooper through all of them, Stephen. I'm very proud of you, son."

I nodded and smiled. "A state trooper?" I asked, cracking a little joke.

"Not exactly," he smiled. Then he grew serious. "The last procedure, exploratory surgery, again confirmed that you have a form of bone cancer—reticular sarcoma. If it's not contained, it will probably invade other parts of your body.

"My team of eight doctors has recommended two different avenues of treatment. Since your condition has been active almost two years with no remission, six of the doctors have voted to amputate your left leg above the knee in the mid-thigh area. That would be about here," he said pointing to the place on the x-ray film.

I could feel the blood draining out of my face. Although my mind was stuck on the word "amputate," I forced myself to keep listening so I wouldn't miss anything.

"They believe this is the safest way to preserve your life," Dr. Colson continued. "Two doctors have chosen intense radiation therapy of your thigh bone area. This is a final attempt to stop the cancer. I make the final decision. You are a strong, determined young man. I can't guarantee that you'll be able to participate in any contact sports, but I'm willing to do a prolonged series of radiation treatments to arrest the cancer. I voted against amputation at this time."

"You don't have to take my leg?" Surprised and relieved at the same time, I gulped air like a drowning swimmer, unaware until then that I'd been holding my breath.

"Not for now, and I hope not ever," the doctor replied.

"Are you sure this is the safer way to go?" Mom gripped my hand harder, and I didn't have to look at her face to know that her reassuring smile had drooped into worry lines.

"Yes, Mrs. Kasperski. Your son is a fighter. Radiation won't be easy, but it *is* a sound option. I will continue to personally supervise Stephen. There will be restrictions, Stephen. No football, not a lot of time in the sun, regular checkups even after the radiation treatments are completed. We need to watch you very closely. No skipping *any* appointments."

"Okay. I won't miss any appointments, even if there's a … blizzard," I promised.

"But maybe . . . just maybe . . . when you improve, those crutches can be put away. Maybe. Any questions?"

"When would he start treatments?" Mom asked.

"This week. Check with my nurse for the schedule."

"Thank you, doctor, thank you so much," my mom said, a quiver in her voice.

"Dr. Colson?" I stood up and put all my weight on my good leg.

"Yes, Stephen?"

"No football?"

"Sorry, son. No football."

"What about fencing?"

The doctor laughed and ruffled my hair. "Who knows, Stephen? Miracles still happen."

Chapter 1
Fifty Years Later

L ate in September, about 5:30 a.m., my sleep was interrupted by a piercing pain in my left leg. Cramps and numbness were everyday companions—even through the night they were common events—but this pain was markedly different. I flexed my calf muscles to ease the tightness. No change.

Hobbling to the bathroom, I switched on the light and examined my leg. *What's going on here?* My leg was usually pale, not fiery red. I took two aspirin, and the pain began to slowly subside. Maybe it was just a really severe cramp. I got back in bed and elevated my leg on a pillow. Resting, but not sleeping, I tried to relax.

At 6:30 a.m., the alarm went off. Before my wife, Bett, got up, I told her about the pain. "We need to see the doctor today," I said.

She called at nine, and they said for me to come right in. The pain was more of an ache by then, but my leg color had changed to blue, almost purple. As Dr. Laurel examined my leg, she seemed concerned; however, I didn't sense any hint of panic, so I figured it was no big deal.

"I want you to go to the hospital today for a Doppler scan, and I'll have Dr. Cato, a vascular physician, read your report."

Her staff called for the appointment, and we were set for 2:00 p.m. at the hospital, fifteen miles west of our home. We went to lunch and then to the hospital. I walked in using my cane, putting the least weight possible on my still-inflamed leg.

The scan revealed two blood clots—one in my thigh and one behind the knee. Blood thinners were an option, but Dr. Cato, the vascular surgeon, was reluctant to let me leave solely on that medication.

The Doppler scan also presented an even more serious condition: a "Triple A" abdominal aneurysm (see Glossary, page 229) bulging on one side, the most dangerous scenario. If this ruptured—and he expected it would within a few months— death would follow almost immediately. He tried to send me to a specialty center in Baltimore eighty miles away, but the "no vacancy" sign was posted. Talk about your life flipping in a matter of hours! It had jumped from a life-changing to a possible life-ending event without warning. Evening was quickly approaching. Because things had happened so fast, we had not contacted any family members or even our pastor.

Within the past two weeks, we had attended the funerals of two dear friends. One died from cancer and the other from an accident. We did not want that same guest list summoned again.

"Don't panic," I said to Bett. "Let's pray." And we did.

Waiting for the doctor, I stepped outside his office at the hospital and smoked what turned out to be my last cigarette. *Can't believe what happened today.* In a flash my future had turned to either uncertain or nonexistent.

Dr. Cato returned and announced the game plan: blood thinners through an IV and a reevaluation in the morning.

Twelve hours ago I didn't even know where this hospital was located because we had moved here only a year ago. For me doctor visits had always been local and uneventful. Now it was 8:00 p.m., and I was in a private room.

About 10:00 p.m., Bett left to find her way home and make some calls. Dr. Laurel, my primary care physician, stopped by to check on me. She reassured me that the vascular surgeon was very well respected and cautious. She agreed with his decision to keep me here with overnight supervision.

Five hours since my last cigarette, my nicotine craving had surfaced. She ordered "the patch," and after it was applied, I began to relax.

Although I did not want to jump ahead of the doctor's blood thinner therapy, at the same time I realized that obviously something was seriously wrong with me. Fifty years ago, as a young boy, I had a form of bone cancer in my upper thigh. Even though treatment at that time was limited to radiation therapy, I had still beaten that obstacle. After mastering the sport of fencing, I had gone on to compete as far as the final round of the Junior Olympics.

Thirty years ago I experienced pain similar to what I had felt this morning—and that was from a blood clot. The remedy for that condition involved taking a vein from my good right leg and inserting it into my left to bypass the clot. I had beaten the odds again. The pain in that instance was much more intense than today's. I hoped and prayed that this warning would have a simple remedy too.

The nurses checked on me several times during the night. I dozed but didn't really sleep. All through the night, I felt an additional presence in the room that projected a warm, safe zone around me. Whether it was an angel—or God Himself— didn't matter to me; I knew I was covered. Different passages of Scripture came to mind, particularly from Psalm 27:1. "The Lord is my light and my salvation, whom shall I fear? The Lord is the strength of my life; of whom shall I be afraid?"

What startled me were the Latin prayers from my altar boy days that popped into my head. *Hey, I'm not ready to go full circle here. It must be the shock and stress from the last twenty-four hours. I'll stay on my current train, thank you very much.* Then I felt that spirit moving about my room again in a flighty fashion. Did I get an angel with a comedic strain? Were all my years of being a bit of a wise guy coming back at me? *Lord, please give me more time.*

"Your wife is on her way up, and Dr. Cato will be here in an hour," the nurse said. What a joy it was to see Bett enter the room. Married twenty-one years, we had encountered many challenges together: dealing with former spouses, step parenting, teenagers, job changes, and the loss of loved ones.

Then the attack on the "Twin Towers," just thirty miles from our home, prompted us to vacate the vulnerable metropolitan area and those difficult memories. Our move last year was in preparation for our retirement. We would work together as a real estate team for another five to seven years in our new location. Knowing that single-floor living—no steps—was better for me, we purchased a ranch-style home. We embraced the simpler life near the soothing ocean surf. It was *our* time.

"How are you feeling, Stephen? Has the doctor been in?" Bett asked.

"Much better, actually. No more pain in the leg. The doctor is due here soon. Did you reach everyone?"

"I got your mom last night, and the kids—Dan and Laura. I called my brothers this morning and the church. I didn't get to call your brother yet. Everyone's praying and hoping you'll be out soon. Dan is going to come tomorrow. Laura will see if she can switch visitation weekends and come too."

"Good. That should cover it for now. I have my brother's number on my cell phone. We can call him later."

"Good morning, Dr. Cato."

"Good morning, Mr. and Mrs. Kasperski. How are you feeling, Mr. Kasperski?"

"Much better since I'm off the leg."

He pressed several places on my leg. "The blood thinner therapy has improved your circulation. We need to continue watching you. I'll be back after my morning appointments."

"Well, that seems to be good news," Bett said after Dr. Cato left the room.

"Yeah, he doesn't seem worried—just cautious," I said.

With that, another person popped into the room. "Hi, there! I saw your name on the patient board and thought I would stop in."

Because he was dressed in green scrubs, I didn't recognize him at first. "Oh, Dr. Light, how are you?"

"Gee, more importantly, how are you?"

"Doing better now. This leg problem started yesterday morning," I said. With that, my podiatrist looked at my leg.

His facial expression rapidly changed from jovial/social to serious/medical.

"Who is your doctor?" Dr. Light asked.

"Dr. Cato."

"Good man who knows his stuff—senior vascular surgeon here. What's his course of action?"

"Blood thinners and reevaluation this afternoon."

"Just tell him I stopped by, and if he needs any of your history, I'll be happy, with your permission, to share it. Right now, I need to check on my patient in recovery."

With that, Dr. Light left.

"He didn't seem too concerned, did he, Bett?"

"No, he just went into serious-doctor mode. But, after all, you're not his patient for this condition. It was nice of him to stop by."

A nurse arrived for more blood work. "Your sugar glucose level is elevated."

An aide delivered my lunch. The menu had most things crossed out. Food with no salt, no fat, and no taste was served . . . with instant Sanka. (I didn't know they still made that stuff.) I mixed the powder in the "hot water," and it changed to a pale brown. I added the skim milk—yuck! Back to water, obviously straight from the tap. They would be checking my blood for chlorine next! *Hopefully, I'll be home for a real dinner tonight.* So, I pushed the food away.

Chapter 2

Just about two p.m. Dr. Cato arrived, this time in blue surgical scrubs. Having checked my lab work results, he examined my leg again.

"Your circulation is still compromised. There's not enough blood flow to your foot. I think we should try to surgically open the clots," Dr. Cato said.

Surgery—this is the real thing. I glanced at Bett, who looked as distressed as I felt. "Is that the only option?" I asked.

He nodded.

"How soon?"

"Within the hour. There's an open operating room, and Dr. Peters, the anesthesiologist, is available. If you agree, we'll begin prepping you immediately. When did you eat last?"

"Breakfast at 7:00 a.m. I didn't eat lunch."

"Okay, we can work with that. Since you've been given a mild sedative, we'll need your wife to sign the surgical permission forms."

Stunned at the news, I managed to say, "What exactly are you going to do? What are the risks and possible complications?"

Touching my leg, he explained, "I will enter the leg above the clots and fish a tube down to open up the artery and break up or push them away. This should allow blood to flow without obstruction."

"Complications?" I asked.

"Any surgery is serious and a shock to the body that could trigger cardiac arrest or a stroke. Do you want life-saving procedures performed or not? Your wife will have to sign."

I looked at Bett, whose eyes were brimming with tears. She nodded yes and reached for my hand. Clasping her hand as I had in so many good and hard times over the past twenty-plus years, I nodded to the doctor. "Okay, let's do it."

"Good," he said and left the room.

Gazing over at Bett, I noticed that the tears were now dripping down her cheeks. She moved closer. "I know you're going to be all right. It's just happening so fast."

And then we hugged tightly.

A nurse team burst into the room and checked my pulse, IV, and the heart monitor. They removed the sensor cups from my leg. A hospital administrator pulled Bett aside and went over the paperwork.

Another nurse arrived. "Say your good-byes. They're ready for you."

We exchanged a quick hug, kiss, and "I love you," and I was on my way to the operating room.

"I'll see you in a couple of hours," Bett called.

Almost flat on the gurney, I felt a gentle breeze, saw fluorescent ceiling lights, and heard the nurses hit door openers. After the last set of double doors opened, monitors came into view all around me. I was in the operating room. Dr. Cato appeared at my side, his surgical mask already in place and eyeglasses covered with a germ barrier.

Acknowledging I was there, he said to the surgical team behind me, "Let's begin."

The IV liquid made me drowsy. A soothing warmth came over me, and I felt gentle hands covering me with a comforter and tucking it in along my sides. *How would they do surgery with that blanket around me?* I drifted out.

"Hi, Stephen—how are things going?" Francine asked. "You remember Harry, the boys' baseball coach?"

In the distance I could see many faces coming toward me.

"Rachel, is that you?" I asked.

"Yes, Stephen, it's me in the flesh—well, almost. How are things in Spring Harbor?"

The whole scene was warm and engaging. Old friends called to me. I felt welcome and unafraid. There was Joe, my tennis buddy. Why hadn't Bett and I kept in touch with these dear ones? Then it struck me—Bett was not with me, and these friends had "crossed over."

I backed away. *What am I doing here?* I had studied the afterlife and believed that the soul continued on, but I wasn't ready to receive my heavenly address. *Get a grip, Stephen. You were just with the doctor. Must be the anesthesia working on you. Just focus on today's events, and you'll be fine.*

"Mr. Kasperski, Mr. Kasperski . . ."

I turned my head. I saw lips moving but could not quite put the words together.

"Mr. Kasperski?"

"Yes," I murmured.

"Do you know where you are?"

I shifted my head to view the room. I saw a row of beds with curtains pulled around several sections. It looked like a medical receiving area. Blinking to verify what was in front of me, I heard someone say, "Mr. Kasperski, do you know where you are?"

"Hospital."

"Right, you're at Amber Memorial Hospital in the recovery room. I'm Angela, your nurse," she said.

Things came back into focus. Blood clots . . . leg . . . surgery.

"Your wife is waiting in our reception area. I'll get her. Dr. Cato will come to see you soon."

I noticed IV packs leading to my arm. Even though a sheet covered my legs, I was still cold but too groggy to ask for a blanket.

"Hello, dear. How do you feel? Any pain?" Bett kissed my cheek.

I reached for her hand, and we touched. What a relief to feel her near me. *The surgery is over. Bett is here, and I'm here.*

Dr. Cato entered, still in his scrubs. "Mr. Kasperski, you're a lucky man. We opened up the clots, and the blood flowed down. The next twenty-four hours are significant. You have a lot of damage to your arterial network, probably from the radiation treatment you had as a child, but there's also plaque in your arteries. Your body has replaced some lines with a new network of capillaries. But we need to watch that your calf and foot stay pink."

With that, he pulled back the sheet, and Bett and I gasped simultaneously. The incision line stretched from my upper thigh to the knee—staples, stitches, and whatever. Not a pretty sight.

"We worked very hard to open everything up. There are several "dead ends" in your circulatory system. I'll be back in a couple of hours to check on you. Any questions?"

"Then, you're pleased with the results? I'll be okay?"

"We opened as much as we could. The clots are opened, but your system is challenged. You're not out of the woods yet. See you later." Dr. Cato left.

"Sounds like mixed signals to me, Bett. What do you think?"

"You know doctors. They always have to give you the worst-case scenario. I'm sure you will be fine."

"I didn't like that 'not out of the woods yet.' What am I—a bear, Goldilocks?"

"Relax, Stephen. You've been through a lot in the last two days. You're a tough cookie, a survivor. You'll be fine," Bett reassured me.

"Your dinner is here," the aide announced. "Amber Memorial's finest."

I looked at the tray: Jell-O, juice, and decaffeinated tea. *Splendid. What I could really use is a cigarette.*

Hushed voices got my attention. Bett stood next to me, and alongside her, Pastor Tom.

"Hey, buddy! How are you doing?"

"Okay," I answered.

"Bett was just telling me that the surgery went well."

"Yes, but I'm still under a twenty-four hour watch."

"That's normal. Everyone experiences different reactions to surgery. Sounds like you did very well."

"I hope so."

Reaching for my hand and Bett's, Pastor Tom said, "Let's pray. Heavenly Father, we thank You for Your servant, Stephen, and his dedication to You. Please be with him, his family, and the medical team as he recovers. We know Your healing touch is the best medicine. In Your precious Son's name, Amen."

"Amen," we said.

"Bett said the family is on the way. It's always good to have everyone rallying around you."

"Yes," Bett said. "Dan should be here tonight, and Laura and Hank tomorrow."

"Maybe I'll be home before the end of the weekend," I said.

"Maybe, but don't push it too much. The doctors know what's best. God bless you both. Good night," Pastor Tom said.

"I should get going, too. Dan should be getting here soon; he left straight from work. Glad you're all right. It's lonely at home without you. Take care. I love you. See you in the morning."

"Love you too, dear. Thanks for everything. I mean *everything.*"

My doctors, the regular one and the surgeon, showed up about 10:00 p.m.

"How are you doing, Mr. Kasperski? How's your pain level?"

"Okay," I responded.

After examining my leg and foot, the doctors said things were good and then left. *It's almost eleven—just let me rest.* As I drifted off to sleep I thought, *No special visitors tonight, please. Let's get life back to normal.*

Morning came, and the blood sampler and pill pusher were making their rounds. One good thing about the Intensive Care Unit is that you have your own space—although not private, of course, with all glass walls facing the nurses' station. "Breakfast" was served: decaffeinated tea, apple juice, and Jell-O. *Where was the real food?*

"Nurse, how about some eggs, cereal, and real coffee like I can smell coming from the nurses' station?"

"Not yet, Mr. Kasperski. The doctor still has you on a post-surgical menu. He'll be in soon. Maybe then you'll get a 'real' lunch," she said.

Ouch! Where did that stabbing pain come from? With this IV and catheter in place, I'm not going anywhere. Let me ring the nurse.

"What do you need, Mr. Kasperski?"

"My pain," I grimaced, "has suddenly increased."

"Between 0-10, with zero being the lowest and ten the highest, what is your pain level?"

"8, 9, 10!" I said.

"The doctor said that we could increase the morphine drip if needed." She adjusted the IV. "You should get relief in five or ten minutes."

I looked at the clock, 9:40 a.m. *The pain should ease by . . . Ow! There's a ten-plus! What's going on here?* I began to feel cold all over. I reached for the call button when Bett entered the room. I saw the startled look on her face and heard her call out.

"Nurse!" Bett shouted.

Quickly surrounded by the ICU staff, I heard voices. I couldn't really grasp what they were saying or doing. The pain had me trembling.

"Stay still, Mr. Kasperski," one said.

"You just had surgery, Mr. Kasperski. You can't get up."

I felt unfamiliar arms across my body, pushing me down. *Who are these people? Why are they holding me? I just want to go out to the deck for a cigarette. I do it every day. What's the big deal?* I pushed back.

"Leave me alone! I know what I'm doing!" I shouted. "You're in my house. Just let me go!"

Then I heard Bett's raised voice. "Stephen, you just had surgery. You can't get up!"

She's with them too. What's happened here? I reached for the tube in my arm to pull it out . . .

With that a large man leaned on my chest and softly whispered, "Stephen, listen to Bett. Listen to these people."

I went limp. When I opened my eyes, everyone was away from the bed. Bett was holding my hand. Her eyes were closed. *Where was the large man?*

"Hello, hon. How are you?" I asked.

Startled, she gazed at me. "Thank goodness you're okay. You gave us quite a scare."

"What do you mean?"

She told me about my trembling and fighting, insisting that I was getting up, and trying to remove IV and other tubes. I had no recollection of those things. She did not mention any large man, but that was all I remembered.

Dan, Laura, and my son-in-law Hank arrived. I was relieved to see them and to have family here for me and Bett. She's been a trooper and my best friend for two decades, but the stress has certainly shaken her. At least she will have the kids at home with her until I'm released.

Dr. Cato arrived and met the rest of the family. He checked the chart and my leg and foot. "I hear you gave the staff a hard time."

"I can't really apologize for what I don't remember, but I'll try to be more cooperative and won't mess up your pretty designs on my leg."

Nodding and smiling, he said, "Good. Your body is fighting for you, Mr. Kasperski. We'll continue to watch your leg a while longer before we make any other decisions. If the blood flow remains open, we'll go in one direction. If it doesn't, the leg will die and be of no use to you. Actually, it will be a threat to you."

"Aren't you encouraged by what you see?" I asked.

"Encouraged, but not convinced. There's still substantial circulatory damage. Time will tell."

"Do you have a 'get me home' timetable?" Bett asked.

"No specific timetable, but the next twenty-four hours remain critical. Good night, everyone."

"He's not very cheery," Hank said.

"Just doing his job, and I've got a good feeling about him," Dan replied.

My two princesses, wife Bett and daughter Laura, remained silent. I did not even want to handle their concerns or my own right then. Hank led us all in prayer, and they left for the night.

As I watched the large clock on the wall, I wished we could turn it back to three days before all this started. *Give me one more peaceful summer afternoon on the deck*, I bargained.

I'll even do without the smokes this time. It's a good life we have here. I'm going to do everything to preserve it "as is."

I felt twinges of pain as I tried to find a comfortable position in the bed, careful not to pull out any of my stitches. The pain was bearable. I could move my toes. *If only I could get some rest.*

Dr. Cato's remarks kept me from relaxing. I knew what he meant by "other decisions." Certainly the blue, almost purple color of my lower leg when he first examined me, prompted a discussion of the possible necessity to remove the leg.

Amputation is a word that startles the bravest of souls. The way you came into this world is the way you want to exit, flailing and kicking, with all body parts intact. As troublesome as my leg has been for fifty years, it is still *my* leg.

Contemplating this scenario was very painful. I was not a healthy young man in the military suffering from a battle wound that resulted in limb loss. My strength level was acceptable, but it wasn't that of someone in their twenties or thirties. *How would I manage without a leg or with an artificial one? How would I be with my wife? How could I enjoy my children and grandchildren?*

"Please, God, keep the blood flowing," erupted from my lips. My outburst startled me. My levels jumped on two of the monitors, but no alarms went off. *Life, death, leg. Leg, death, life.* I'm not ready for those choices.

With that, alarms went off in the adjacent cubicle. Staff hurried in and began checking the systems. From the words I could make out, it sounded like the patient had rolled over onto some of the monitor lines and set them off. Things quieted down. I was happy for the other patient, as well as happy for myself that I was not setting off any alarms.

Try to rest, Stephen, maybe sleep. Think about some happier times. That always works in the dentist's chair. Let's try it here. My last thought before sleeping was of last Thanksgiving morning, seated in the bleachers at the high school football game with a cup of hot chocolate in my hand and my arm around Bett. It had begun to snow. We were shivering and yet warm under the blanket. The good life. *Angels, keep watching over me. Good night, my special guardians.*

Chapter 3

Morning comes very early in the ICU—there is always activity. My liquid breakfast was in front of me by 6:45 a.m.—apple juice, Jell-O, broth, and lukewarm tea. *Better than nothing.* I finished it all.

My regular physician was off for the weekend, so Dr. Cato would be solely in charge. Even after just knowing him for a few days, I liked his manner, respected his handiwork, and trusted his cautious handling of my situation. He had been a vascular surgeon for more than thirty years and even did some hospital field work for the Army, so I imagined he had seen it all.

Daydreaming after eating, I was awakened by the sensation of someone touching my leg.

"Good morning, Mr. Kasperski."

"Good morning, Dr. Cato."

"How did you sleep? Any major pain episodes?" he asked.

"I slept a few hours. No big pain, just twinges from the staples pulling."

"Good," he said.

With that, he pulled a small machine over to my bed. "This is a portable Doppler scan. I need to take a reading of your circulation."

Beep, beep, beep, as he ran it over my upper leg.

Beep . . . beep . . . silence as he went farther down my leg. He tried it again from the other side. No noise. He pressed behind my knee, and there was only minimal sensation. He went even farther down my leg. There was no noise, no sensation. He tried again—same result.

"Is your wife here?" he asked.

"No. She should be here in an hour," I said.

After turning off the machine with the two of us inside the draped area, he said, "Mr. Kasperski, the news is not good. Your leg is dying. What we had opened up with the surgery has closed down again. I am worried that more clots could form and move through your body. If that happens, there would not be enough time to save you. I believe we need to take the leg right away."

A rush of shock and disbelief hit me. I didn't move or respond.

"Mr. Kasperski, did you understand what I just told you?" Dr. Cato asked.

"Yes," I murmured. "Can't you try one more time to open everything up?"

"You've been on borrowed time here for the past few days. I really feel we need to take action today to head off any more clots moving through your body. It's dangerous to wait. I know this is a shock to you. Discuss it with your family, but I need an answer this morning—two hours, tops."

I nodded.

He touched my shoulder and said, "Sorry," and left.

The drape was still drawn when Bett and the rest of the family arrived. Hank and Dan were playfully pushing and shoving each other around when Laura pulled back the drape. They gasped as they saw the purplish color of my leg. Bett reached for my hand and leaned in to give me a hug.

No words came out of my mouth.

"What happened, dear? You look so distant and pale. Was the doctor here today?"

"He wants to take my leg," I managed to get out.

"What?" Dan questioned.

"No way!" Hank affirmed.

"Daddy," Laura came to me, with tears already in her eyes.

With that, Dr. Cato came back into the room. "Good morning, everyone. We have done everything that was safe to do and waited as long as we could. The leg is dying. If any of these clots move, we cannot be sure of his survival. I'm sorry. I strongly recommend surgery—today. I'll be back after I see two other patients." And then he was gone.

Silence.

"What are you going to do, Dad?" Dan asked.

"We're here for you, Dad—whatever you decide," Hank said.

"I know it's my decision, but I need to speak to Bett alone."

"Okay, Daddy. I love you." Laura hugged me. I felt her tears and mine as our cheeks touched.

In a group they filed out, soberly and quietly.

"I haven't had much time to process what he's asking," Bett said.

"I know—me either. But I've had almost fifty years with this leg, from the time when 'taking it' almost happened with the cancer. I know it's not perfect, but it has served me a long time. Our lives will change so much. Are you ready for that, Bett?"

"I don't think anyone could be prepared for what has happened in the past seventy-two hours. One thing I do know is that *you* are not your leg. We need to do everything we can to save *you*. God will give us the strength. He always has."

"What about a second opinion? From the beginning, Dr. Cato has been trying to get me moved to a larger research hospital. Maybe they'll have another option, a new technique."

"Do you feel there's time for that? He seems convinced that surgery needs to be done right away."

"For my own peace of mind, I want to explore that option. I'm the one who has to live with this loss of limb. If that has to be . . . well, I need to exhaust every possibility, every chance."

Bett just nodded and came closer to me, wrapping her arm under mine. Hank poked his head in the room. I waved to him to come in. They all surrounded my bed.

"I've decided to get a second opinion. I need to know that amputation, a word I did not ever want to hear, is my *only* choice."

"Do you think it's wise to wait?" Dan asked.

"Is it safe for you to wait, Daddy?" Laura asked.

Dr. Cato entered. "Are we ready?"

"With all that is at stake here, for me and my family, I really want a second opinion," I said.

"I can appreciate that this decision is very difficult, but I do need to emphasize that we are fighting the clock here. You may be limiting, rather than expanding, your choices. I've tried to reach the hospital again today that I would recommend, but there's still no room. Other places near here are similar in size and staff. I'm sure they would offer the same directive that I have. Plus, it's the weekend when staff is always light."

"It's not that I don't trust your opinion. I just need to know."

"Okay, let me try another city hospital. They do have a very well-known vascular team there. I'll be back shortly."

There was complete silence in the room. Bett motioned everyone to gather closer. With our arms interlocked and each one of them touching me, she began to pray.

"Father, You know how much we love Stephen. Please shelter him and keep him safe. Be with the doctors. Be with all of us, each one covered in Your loving care. We need Your help and intervention. In Jesus' name, Amen."

As we opened our eyes, we saw that Dr. Cato was already in the room. Nurses were behind him. "I reached an assistant to the top vascular surgeon. They're on call this weekend. I explained your situation. They'll be waiting for you. We need to get you going! Stat! Okay?"

"Okay, let's do it!" I responded with conviction.

Nurses began preparing me for travel: Blankets. Portable IV. Oxygen tank. Chart near my feet. They directed the family to take my personal items and handed Bett directions to the hospital.

It was eighty miles to my next stop, and there was no room in the ambulance for Bett. A nurse would be in there with me and the EMT. Two really large ambulance drivers arrived and began rolling me out of my room. We raced through the corridors and doors crashed open. They shoved the gurney through the rear doors of the truck-like vehicle. With lights flashing and sirens blaring, we took off.

I felt the vehicle moving faster and faster. I was not expecting such urgency. Maybe I had underestimated how much "time" I had. *Too late to turn back now.* Bam! We hit a bump, and my body momentarily bounced on the stretcher. Everything hurt at once. *What a ride!*

The EMT called to the driver, "No more like that one."

"Sorry, but the doc said STAT."

Time seemed both long and short inside that vehicle. The attendant was constantly checking my readings.

"How do you feel, Mr. Kasperski?" the nurse asked.

"Okay. Quick, stabbing pain sometimes."

The EMT stared into my eyes. "Your pain level?"

"Eight when they hit. Does it have to be so warm in here?"

The attendants looked at each other. "How far out are we?" the EMT yelled to the driver.

"Ten, fifteen minutes."

"Make it ten."

I sensed that we picked up speed. *No more bumps, please. I don't know if I can take it.*

"Big turn coming up. Oops, pothole. Hold on."

Bam!

Suddenly Bett, Mom, and my brother Paul were around me. We were at the Blakely Restaurant, and someone was bringing a cake to the table.

"Happy birthday, Stephen," Bett said.

"Another year older, pal," Paul offered.

"How can my son be this old? Makes me feel ancient."

"Birthday boys get served first. Make a wish, dear."

Preparing to blow out the candles, I heard voices around me.

"Lift on three. One, two, lift." I sensed I was both floating and dropping. *Ouch! What was that?* I opened my eyes.

"Mr. Kasperski, good to have you back. Sorry for the rough ride."

Looking around, I saw unfamiliar faces. A nurse looked down at me.

"You did well, Mr. Kasperski. I thought Gene was going to make all of us airborne inside the ambulance! Do you know where you are?"

"Not sure. Another hospital?"

"Right. You're in the ER at Trinity Hospital, Baltimore. We're turning you over to them."

"Good afternoon, Mr. Kasperski. How are you feeling? I'm Dr. Andwar.

I'm just going to check your leg. Your surgery was done yesterday?"

"Yes, I think so."

He pulled a machine over, put some gel on the sensors, and began to run it up and down my leg. It was my third or maybe fourth time with this machine. I knew what he was doing.

Beep . . . silence. Beep . . . silence.

"Ouch!"

"Sorry, Mr. Kasperski. I needed to probe near the incision." As he went down my leg, he asked, "What sensation do you have here?"

"Tightness," I responded.

"Any pain?"

"No."

"Here?" he asked as he pushed with his fingers near my lower calf and ankle.

"None."

"Here?" pressing on the side of my foot.

"None."

"Mr. Kasperski, I cannot find a pulse in your ankle or foot. The circulation is minimal at best. Your leg is dying. There's no choice but to remove it above the clot."

"Dr. Cato opened up the clots."

"I imagine that was his goal, but now we have to go above the thigh clot where there is healthy tissue to make it safe for you."

He touched my leg above my old bypass scar. He was almost all the way up my leg. "Up there?!"

"Yes, we need to get above your radiated tissue. Your bypass has failed. We cannot rely on that to carry the blood needed to keep the tissue below alive. Dr. Cato did all that he could. I concur with his diagnosis."

This had to be my darkest hour—alone in this big city hospital, confronted by a medical stranger telling me he needed to take my leg, leaving me with no other option. This was too much, and I began sobbing.

"Mr. Kasperski, are you okay? Let me give you a minute by yourself." He opened and closed the drape around my stretcher and left.

I looked at my leg—cut open, stapled back together, mottled and purple, yet still mine. Maybe this was the end of the trail for me. *What would I do? Could I live with one leg? What would life be like? Could I survive?* Feeling chilled again, I pulled up the sheet.

Bett's voice broke the somber silence. "Can you tell me where Stephen Kasperski is?"

"Did he come in here by ambulance?" the receptionist asked.

"Yes, he was referred here from Amber Memorial."

"He's in cubicle two, behind there. The doctor was just with him."

"Hello, dear. We got here as quickly as we could. We lost half an hour just trying to get past Oriole Stadium. Looks like the whole Red Sox nation is in town to see the game. How are you doing?"

"What's the news, Dad?" Dan inquired.

"Daddy, what did the doctor say?" Laura asked.

"They still want to take my leg." My voice trembled. "Looks like we all made this trip for nothing."

"Don't they have any other suggestions—a bypass or something?" Hank asked.

"You had to get a second opinion, dear," Bett said. "You needed to be sure if amputation was your only option, and now you know."

Gesturing in agreement, I could feel my emotions ready to spill out of me again.

"Hello, everyone," Dr. Andwar said, returning with a colleague. "This is Dr. Davids, chief of surgery."

"Good afternoon, everyone. Let's see what we have here."

With that he pulled back the sheet. I heard several gasps as the family stepped back. Blood was streaming out of the staples near my ankle and above my knee. *What happened?* Both of the doctors grabbed gloves and began to apply pressure.

"Ow!" I yelped.

"Sorry, sir, but we need to get this stopped." I saw alarm in Dr. Davids' eyes. "Nurse! Family, please step out!"

My knuckles turned white as I clutched Bett's hand. She began peeling my fingers away. The last thing I wanted to do was let her hand go. Another stabbing pain. Instinctively, I tightened my grip.

"Stephen, please let go of my hand. I need to get out of the doctors' way," Bett pleaded. I looked at Bett, her eyes frightened and anguished. The pain spike was subsiding. My hand opened. "I'll be right outside here with the kids," she said.

The doctors' hands and arms blocked my view. I felt wraps being tightened around my leg.

Chills.

Pain.

Chills.

I'm in big trouble now. Trembling took over. *Oh God, please save me.*

I am not my leg.

I am not my leg.

Take my leg. Save me.

"Mr. Kasperski, do you know where you are?" a nurse asked.

"Hospital. Baltimore."

Bett reentered the room.

"Mr. Kasperski, we need to prep you for surgery. We need to remove your leg right away before the clots move or bleeding resumes. Either problem could take your life. Do you agree to have the surgery?" Dr. Andwar asked.

"Yes, I do," I murmured.

"Say again."

"Yes," I said.

"We need you to sign the surgical permission papers."

I nodded.

Papers were put in front of me for my signature. Hands still trembling, I signed. I knew what I was agreeing to, but it almost felt as if I were doing this for someone else. It was too much to process, too fast.

"We'll give you five minutes with your family," a voice murmured. All the medical staff left.

Laura, Hank, and Dan came in. They instinctively formed a close circle, hugging and touching me and one another. Tears were everywhere. No macho moments now.

"I love you, Daddy," Laura whispered.

"You're strong, Dad," Hank affirmed.

"We're here for you, Dad," Dan said.

"The Lord is here," Bett said. "Please be with Stephen and guide the doctors' hands. Our Father, who art in heaven . . . Thine is the kingdom, the power, and the glory forever. Amen," we all prayed together.

One more hug, and I was on my way, into the elevator and moving quickly down a corridor. Big doors opened. Bright lights above me flooded my vision.

"Mr. Kasperski, I'm Dr. Benson, your anesthesiologist. I'm going to begin the anesthesia. Please count backward from 100 when I ask. Do you understand?"

"Yes." Fighting unconsciousness, I wanted to think about my family one more time. Picturing us all together moments ago was soothing. It was comforting to know they were nearby. *I will see them soon. I will wake up.*

"Start counting backward from 100," a voice instructed.

"100, 99, 98, 97, 96, what's next? 95 . . . 94 . . .

Chapter 4

F eeling chilled, I reach for the blanket. *Did Bett steal the covers again? Good thing I'm warm blooded. I could really use a blanket tonight. At least I have a sheet to cover me. Why is it so bright in here? Is it morning already?*

More drifting.

Opening my eyes, I see tubes running from my arm. My other arm has a blood pressure cuff on it. Looking farther down my body, I see there is only one bump at the end of the bed.

Oh, no! I only have one foot. The thought of what had just happened to me made me feel sick to my stomach. How could I have agreed to have a part of my body severed? And so high up! *A quarter of my body is gone. I am a freak! How can I live like this? This is just too much!* I closed my eyes very tight, like a child pretending to be asleep. Shaking from the shock, I tried to push all thoughts away.

Suddenly, without request, I felt a warm calm come over me, and a buffer of peace surrounded me.

"Stephen, My child, you are safe now. Heed My helpers. We are all with you."

I heard the voice so clearly. I opened my eyes to see who was in the room—no one, just machines. I looked again. Recovery area. No TV, no radio. I heard the voice I needed to hear. *God is here.* With that assurance, I peacefully closed my eyes.

Hearing muffled voices, I began to stir. I sensed a familiar touch as I opened my eyes. Bett had her arm under my forearm and was holding my hand. I squeezed her hand in acknowledgement. Our eyes met as she leaned over to kiss me. Feeling her nearby comforted me.

Laura's face came into view. "Thank God you're safe, Daddy."

"Yes, I'm safe. I'm not going anywhere." We hugged one another.

"How do you feel, Dad?" Dan asked.

"I'm okay, son," I responded.

"Everyone has been praying for you, Dad. We must have five states in the loop," Hank said.

"Tell them I'm fine, and the prayers are appreciated."

Dr. Andwar stepped in. "How are you doing, Mr. Kasperski? How is your pain level?"

"I feel good. No severe pain."

"Good. Often there is not severe pain with an amputation. Your body knew the leg was bad and dangerous for you to keep. You will probably experience phantom pain for six months to a year, or even longer at your age. Your mind has had two legs all your life. It will be looking for your leg, and the pain of your condition may linger. Let's check the surgery."

He gestured for the family to leave. They filed out rapidly. *Gee, I want to leave, too. I'm not ready to see . . . my leg.*

He closed the drape and put on gloves. Lifting the sheet on my left side, he leaned toward me and lightly touched my leg.

"How does your stump feel? Much pain?" he asked.

I did not respond. It was not pain that stopped me from speaking—it was the word "stump." I no longer had a leg, just a stump. That reality hit hard.

"We had to go higher than expected. We needed to get above the irradiated dead tissue. I am afraid there's not much to work with. Much pain?"

I shook my head no.

"Good. I'll check on you again in a few hours."

Stump. Not much to work with. I lifted the sheet again and reached down. *Six to seven inches at best. This is going to be much tougher than I thought.* Decisions had been made so quickly. I hoped I did the right thing—not that there was really any other choice. The clot happened. The doctor tried to open it and reintroduce healthy oxygen-filled blood to the leg and foot, but that had failed. *I need to keep focused on the bigger picture. I am here—minus a limb—but still here.*

Chapter 5

An aide pushed my stretcher into the room. There, I met Al and his wife. Al was obviously in a lot of pain. His wife was trying to make him as comfortable as possible. I was relieved that they were too preoccupied to ask what had happened to me. I did not think I could say "amputation" just yet.

The nursing staff took Al for some tests, and his wife went with him. I tried to doze, but finding a comfortable position was extremely difficult. With lines connected to a monitor, suction cups attached to my chest, plus an IV pumping something into me, I only had limited ways to turn.

Bett came into the room. I was struck by her pale complexion and the dark circles under her eyes. With everything focused on me for the last several days, I had missed these changes in my spouse. My Bett, my anchor, had embraced my pain. I reached for her hand and drew her near to me.

"How are you, dear?"

"Okay. Thankful that you're still here," she said.

"Where are the kids?"

"We got rooms at a hotel two blocks away. They always keep some rooms available for family members of patients. I told them I wanted to get back to you. We had a light supper. Did you get any food yet?"

"Not yet. But it's coming. Some real food—well, hospital real food. I've had enough Jell-O for a while."

"It's great that you're so alert and your appetite and personality are back," she said.

"Did it go away?"

"The fever and the pain had you for a while. You were rambling on about a Yankees game, implying that the pitcher was left in too long. Then you got silly about one of the nurses being too familiar with you. It was strange. You were here, yet separated from the serious situation—logical and in control of your choices, but in a whole different place."

"I remember making one really big choice," I said.

"Yes, you made that decision. I was glad that you were able to make it. The doctors told me that if you blanked out from the fever or they gauged you were incoherent, I would have had to sign the surgery papers."

"I know you would have done what was necessary," I said.

I felt her shared pain and love as we gazed into one another's eyes. No words were necessary.

"Better go before it gets dark," I said. "Get some rest."

"Okay. Miss you. Love you. See you in the morning."

My supper came. Food at last: soup, mashed potatoes, bread, and cranberry juice. *I'll take it. Now, if I could only go out for a smoke. Maybe in the morning. I guess that patch thing is working. Lose a leg and stop smoking all at the same time. I wonder if anyone has ever done that! Bett's right . . . my personality is returning.*

Chapter 6

"Hey man, what are you doing?" Al questioned me.

"Just going to the bathroom."

Nurses flew into the room. "Mr. Kasperski, what are you doing getting up?"

"I had to go to the bathroom like I do every night," I protested. With that, I realized I was on a cold floor.

Hands were locked under my arms. "On the count of three. One, two, three." I was lifted onto the bed. *Clang!* The side rail of the bed went into place.

"You stay right where you are, Mr. Kasperski. Call a nurse when you need to go to the bathroom. We'll get a doctor to check your surgery sutures."

"You gave us some scare," Al's wife said.

"I guess I was sleeping. I knew that I had to go to the bathroom and just started to get up. I forgot that I didn't have two legs. I guess the nurses thought I was too groggy to move."

"Are you okay?" Al asked.

"I think so. No major pain, mostly ego damage. I guess I shocked everyone."

A member of the surgical team arrived and checked me. All the stitches and staples were okay. As I reflected on what had just happened, two things struck me. Years of having a weak leg had actually protected me. Whether I was naturally left or right footed, I had become right leg dominant. Alert or groggy, I always knew to put the right leg down to be the load-bearing limb, allowing the weaker left to follow. Now it was a whole new ballgame. The right was dominant, but solo. This old dog needed to learn some new ways to find mobility.

Fifty years with a bum leg, and I still had my independence. Calling someone because I needed to go to the bathroom was not my style. I did not want it to *be* my style, either. Recovery from surgery was the immediate issue, but restructuring my life held an even bigger challenge. This first lesson was a big one: amputation is not for wimps.

Chapter 7

My Tuesday night "free fall" was the talk of the ninth floor the next day. Was I Spiderman, Superman, or the one-legged character in *The Fugitive II?* It was good to laugh and be teased about my late-night adventure. I think even my angels got a chuckle over my "stepping out" attitude.

However, the hospital administrator was quick to visit me. Having the sidebar down after surgery was a major safety issue.

As for me, my focus was on moving forward to the best of my ability, not in pointing blame.

When would my rehabilitation therapy start? Wednesday? Good.

I wanted to move forward with my life. These new bonus days, hopefully years, would be precious.

Chapter 8

"Hi, Dad. How are you doing?" Dan said as he sat in the chair beside my bed. "You gave us some scary days. Let's try to do some more 'normal' things together when you're out of here, like a ball game. We're really close to the Orioles' stadium. The Yankees are coming to town today. Are you up for a game? Bet you I could get some tickets, especially since it's the last week of the season."

"I think I need to pass on that for now, Dan. Let's schedule an outing for the spring. More time together is a good plan, though."

"Hank and I were talking about 'bringing' a Yankee to you. After all, you are a faithful fan. You watch all the games, even the late night ones from the West Coast."

"What do you mean by 'bringing'?" I asked.

Dan sheepishly responded, "You know, encouraging a player to visit here since you can't go there."

"Let's skip your well-intentioned Jersey way of bringing someone here."

"We weren't going to 'acquisition' one of the superstars, maybe just one of the short-reliever bullpen guys."

"Who thought of this idea, you or Hank?"

"Well, with all the Red Sox fans around here these last few days, it was just getting to us. I think we both came up with this special "Father's Day-in-September" gift at the same time," Dan said proudly.

"Well, I think next spring or that traditional Father's Day in June will be fine for a baseball outing for all of us. Let's keep the Yankees in 'pinstripes,' not you two in jail pinstripes."

"Are you sure, Dad?"

"I'm sure. Thanks for the thought, though."

"Not even a coach?"

"No, Dan, we're good."

"Okay."

With that, Bett, Laura, and Hank arrived. "Dad nixed the Yankee idea," Dan said.

"We just wanted to borrow one or two players. Maybe they would want to come see you," Hank added.

"I think with the playoffs starting next week, they're pretty busy. I'm happy just to see the games on TV right now. Did you know about this, Bett?"

"Boys will be boys. I suggested e-mailing the front office, just in case maybe the designated hitter was available."

"You're too much." Appreciation welled up within me as I smiled at them.

Bett spoke up. "Well, we all needed a little emotional R&R, dear."

"Amen."

Chapter 9

Being pushed in a wheelchair from place to place was a new experience for me. First, my viewing perspective was from a different, shorter level. Second, I was not used to having my movement controlled by someone else. In a hospital, of course, there are many folks in wheelchairs. Insurance regulators and post-surgical conditions require it. My strength level at the moment welcomed the assistance. I was being guided to the fourth floor for my first physical therapy experience since the amputation.

How would I manage with one leg? What would I be asked to do? What would my pain level be? I certainly didn't want to come down on my stump or meet the floor suddenly again. I said a prayer, asking for strength and help through the next hour.

I counted six patients as I entered the room. Most of them—older than I—used walkers or were having their muscles stretched; however, nobody showed physical pain by their facial expressions, but it wasn't a happy atmosphere, either. Hip replacements, knee replacements, stroke rehabilitation—whatever the need, it was being addressed.

Suddenly, reality hit me. I was the only one minus a limb. Even with my double hospital gown and blanket on my lap, I had two footrests but only needed one. I felt compromised and sad. Grief swept over me. Even though my personality was intact, my body was not.

"Mr. Kasperski, how are you doing? Ready to get started? I'm Michael, your therapist for today."

I nodded.

"We'll start first with some upper-body stretching. Take these weights and lift them above your head twelve times, like this, doing one arm at a time. Ready?"

"Okay."

The upper-body exercise I could manage.

"Hey, that's good. Good job, Mr. Kasperski. Now, have you been standing since your surgery?"

"Once, briefly," I said.

"Good, we'll do that next," Michael said.

I've been standing since I was ten months old, but now it was an exercise—an exercise that I wasn't sure I was ready to do.

Michael placed a walker in front of me. "We're going to have you stand, Mr. Kasperski—not walk, just stand. Are your wheels locked?"

"Wheels locked?" I asked.

"On the wheelchair—are your wheels locked? We need you to push your body up with your arms. Then reach one hand at a time for the walker."

Feeling for the side of the chair, I reached for the lever and pushed it forward into the hard rubber-faced wheels. First I locked the right, then the left. Not much time to ponder this new experience with Michael waiting in front of me, but I appreciated the necessity of doing this correctly. I didn't want the chair to scoot away from me. Balancing on one leg would be short lived.

"The wheels are locked," I reported.

"Good. Now push up with your arms."

As I began pushing up, Michael balanced himself at an angle in front of me, raising his arms in almost "stop sign" fashion to guard me against a fall.

"Good. Now reach for the walker, right side first. Bring your left hand over immediately so as to not tip over the walker."

As quick as that, I was standing. It felt good to do this for myself, and to be out of the chair.

"Now let's try to stand for one minute, Mr. Kasperski."

One minute? Who does he think he's talking to? I used to stand for nine hours in my retail days. But I felt my strength draining rapidly. My head felt light.

"Just sit back, Mr. Kasperski. I've got you. You won't fall."

With that, I collapsed backwards and slammed into the wheelchair seat. My skin was clammy, my strength evaporated.

"Would you like some water, Mr. Kasperski? You did well. We'll give you a five-minute rest and do it again."

Do it again? Not today, buddy.

Michael began making notations on a chart—my medical history of physical therapy.

Bett and Laura appeared in the room. "Are you okay, Daddy? You look pale."

"He did well. I'm Michael, his therapist. Let's show your family what you can do."

Center stage and on the spot, I braced to perform.

"Wheels locked?"

Reaching to check, I answered, "Yes."

He checked the placement of the walker and said, "Stand."

Ready and praying at the same time, I pushed myself up with my arms and grabbed the walker. Standing, I looked at my cheering section. The girls were hugging one another with eyes ready to overflow with tears of joy.

"That's wonderful," Bett said.

"Awesome, Daddy!" Laura exclaimed.

"Good job, Mr. Kasperski. You're done for today. You have a new job tomorrow—walking."

Chapter 10

Isettled back in my room, ready for a well-deserved rest. I chilled out with the TV on for background noise. Just as I was beginning to doze off, Dr. Andwar arrived.

"How are you doing, Mr. Kasperski? On a scale of 1-10, with 1 being the lowest and 10 the highest, what is your pain level?"

"About 3," I responded.

"Good. Let me check your stump." He lifted the sheet.

Can't they get more "patient friendly" by using terms like "remaining limb" or "surviving left leg"? "Stump" sounds so blunt—so isolated and dormant.

"It looks good. Healing nicely."

With that, another person in scrubs arrived. "Mr. Kasperski, I'm Dr. Lukas. I will be doing your Triple A surgery to repair your aneurysm. We have scheduled you for Friday morning, the day after tomorrow. We'll run blood work on you again tomorrow and do a final scan so we can measure exactly the size sheath we need to contain the bulge in your blood vessel. We have various sizes here, but we want to be sure we're ready for you."

Dr. Lukas leaned closer and looked directly into my eyes. "Good to meet you, Mr. Kasperski. Let me just reassure you that even though you're having the less invasive surgical procedure, we have had great success with this technique over the last twelve years. There is less bleeding and a much faster recovery time with this method. With your recent amputation, we want to reduce your blood loss and minimize the shock to your body. I will do two small incisions in your lower stomach and work from there. The procedure usually takes less than an hour. Do you have any questions? Do you have any family here?"

"No questions. Just take good care of me. This is my third surgery in less than ten days. My wife and daughter are here."

"You'll be fine, Mr. Kasperski. It's very important that you get this done. Your case is particularly dangerous with the artery bulging on one side. Here's a booklet about the procedure. I'll speak to your family in the waiting area afterward."

The two doctors left.

Surgery number three. I'm more scared and nervous about this one. If the aneurysm ruptures, I'm out of here. *Lord, be with me and guide the doctors. Be with my family and hold them close. I need to get through Friday.* I closed my eyes. *I need to get through Friday.*

For the first time in almost a week, I was worried that my time on this earth was coming to a rapid countdown. All surgery is risky. You always have to sign those "check-out-could-happen" forms. *If I only have twenty-four hours left, what do I need or want to do?*

I didn't like thinking so negatively. My positive, faith-driven approach to life had carried me through many physical and emotional trials before. What was different this time?

It was time for a reality check—the only practical thing to do. I needed to say some personal things to Bett and Laura. They should hear what I had to say from my lips instead of assuming something through penetrating eye contact. I knew they knew I loved them, but I needed to tell them what they meant to me. I didn't want to frighten them—just offer my peace.

In a minute. I'll talk to them in a minute. In a minute . . .

Chapter 11

"The peace of Christ be with you."

"And also with you," I responded. Opening my eyes, I saw my pastor in front of me. *Pastor!? Where were the girls? I was going to talk to them . . .*

"Hi, Stephen. How are you feeling?" Tom said.

"Okay. Good to see you, Tom." We clasped hands.

"Bett has been keeping me informed of your condition. I did come to see you before your surgery, but you were pretty much out of it. I don't know if you remember that."

"Not really."

"What progress have you made?"

"I started therapy yesterday. I was able to balance myself and stand."

"Good for you! Bett mentioned that you have one more surgery. Has that been scheduled?"

"Yes, it's Friday."

"That's tomorrow," Tom said.

"You do get your days mixed up in here. Right, it's tomorrow."

"Do you know when?"

"In the morning, I think."

"I need to be with another family tomorrow, but I'll speak with Bett and check up on you."

"Thank you, Pastor."

"Many members have been calling and asking about your progress and are praying for you. Through e-mail, the prayer committee has gotten any new information right away. You have many Christian sisters and brothers praying for you."

"Thank you. I can feel their concern and support. My son-in-law, Hank, tells me that there are people praying in five different states. That is very humbling for me."

"You are a man of great faith and are well loved, Stephen. Before we pray, is there anything else I can do for you?"

"Yes, Pastor. I need to talk to you about contingency plans."

"Contingency plans?"

"I know my body has had many shocks in the past few days. I'm not looking to be negative, but in case I don't wake up, I want to share a few things with you."

"Okay."

"I'm concerned that Bett will be lonely and isolated. We've made friends in the past year, but they aren't yet the deep friendships we had before. Maybe you could ask one of the ladies to check on her once a week and take her out—or just have 'girl talk' over tea."

"We do have some very warm and caring members who could help out, if needed. It's important that you go into tomorrow with hope, not defeat or high anxiety about your family."

"I know that, Pastor, but my comfort zone and hope will be strongly enhanced if I know you can cover this request. I want that 'special person' to be there if I can't."

"I'll take care of it."

"Thank you. I feel better. Whether I'm here or somewhere else, I have no worries about my care. I know that I *feel* God so close to me these days. I'm not angry over my loss. I'm thankful to have come this far with family and angels around me."

"Angels?"

"Yes, I have a couple who make themselves known to me. One is actually a bit of a wise guy!"

"A wise guy?"

"You're too young to remember the TV show, "Topper." The two angels who show up—George and Marion Kirby—can only be seen by Topper."

"I don't know the TV show, but I have seen the black-and-white movie," Tom said.

"Well, sometimes my angels laugh and even pick on me. You know that I stopped smoking?"

"Yes, good for you."

"Well, I think one angel was holding a cigarette in his hand. I could even smell the smoke."

"Stephen, you can always make me laugh."

"No, really."

"Well, we know our Lord has a sense of humor, but angels smoking? I think it's time to pray. Why don't you start, and I'll close."

"Okay. Heavenly Father, for Your loving hands, I thank You. For the gift of a good medical team, I thank You. For Bett, Laura, Hank, Dan, and Mom, brothers and sisters—all the family, thank You. For Your greatest gift, Your Son, for Your presence in our lives, for the Holy Spirit to comfort and hold me—for my life—thank You."

Pastor Tom continued, "Gracious God, we give thanks for your servant, Stephen, and caring for his every need. For his loving wife and family, sustain them, Lord, and be with them. For all the doctors, nurses, and staff caring for Stephen during tomorrow's procedure, we ask that You stay beside the team and guide them while You hold Stephen, safe and confident, in Your hands. For we know that You are the Great Physician, and You are in charge. We feel Your Spirit, Lord. What a wonderful gift. We love You and thank You for being with us and allowing us to worship You. In the name of the Father, the Son, and the Holy Spirit, Amen.

"God bless you, Stephen. You have been a witness to so many. See you Saturday."

"Thank you, Pastor. Until then . . ."

Chapter 12

"Good morning, Mr. Kasperski. We need to get you to the operating room for your procedure an hour earlier than expected. I will be back shortly with the transport team," the nurse informed me.

"Good morning, dear. When I called the nurses' station at 6:30 this morning, they said you were going earlier. I came as quickly as I could," Bett said.

Reaching for each other, we shared a long embrace. Our eyes communicated both our anxiety and love simultaneously.

"How are you feeling, Stephen?"

"Sleepy at the moment. No real pain."

Good. That's a blessing. You've been through so much. Your strength keeps me going," Bett said.

"Just having you here with me keeps me going. I love you, Bett."

"I love you too."

As we embraced, the staff entered the room.

"They're ready for you, Mr. Kasperski. We need to get going," the nurse said.

I looked over at Bett, and her head was already bowed in prayer. The IV was being transferred to a different pole and sheets were pulled up to cradle me, creating a hammock effect.

"On three," the aide said, "one, two, three." At once I was lifted out of the bed and placed onto a narrow rolling cart. Out of the room we flew!

"I'll see you in a little while," I heard Bett say.

They rolled me down the corridor and into the elevator. I could feel the upward movement, and we stopped at the ninth floor. The elevator door opened, and we made a quick turn. The orderly hit the wall plate, and I saw two large doors open. Ready or not, I was here.

"Good morning, Mr. Kasperski. How are you feeling?" A mask-covered face addressed me.

"Good, doctor."

"Okay, we're ready to get started. We'll give you something to make you drowsy, but not heavy general anesthesia. I'll speak with you and your family after we're done. Any questions? Now, start counting backwards from 100," Dr. Lukas said.

Questions? Just one. Will I make it? How much can this beat-up body take? Think positive. Feeling warm and suddenly calm . . . the Spirit is here.

"Start counting," a distant voice commanded.

"100, 99, 98 . . . 97."

I heard a voice speaking to me.

"Come on, Stephen, we need to get going. The game is starting in ten minutes . . . ."

"I'll be right there, Jeff. Just need to grab my jacket."

Climbing into the SUV, I buckled my belt. "Ready."

"Stephen, where's your leg? How did you get over here?" Jeff asked.

Looking down at myself, I realized . . .

"Mr. Kasperski, are you awake?" the nurse said. "It's time to wake up."

I turned my head and opened my eyes in the direction of her voice. A woman wearing a blue cap adjusted my IV. "There you are, Mr. Kasperski. Wake up. The doctor is coming to see you."

With mask off but cap still on, I saw the surgeon. "It went very well, Mr. Kasperski. We have your artery contained. It was a large bulge, but the sheath is in place to prevent any rupture. It was good that we got you here when we did. I will check on you tomorrow, but if all is well, you should be able to go home on Monday. Any questions? I will see your family now and tell them what I told you."

All the strain and emotional stress of the past nine days suddenly hit me. My watery eyes released tears and my body trembled.

"You're okay," the nurse encouraged me. "Is anything hurting you?"

I did a mental body check and shook my head. Tears were replacing words right now. *What a relief to be here. I will have more time with my family. Now I can plan for the days to come. I made it to Friday.*

"Thank You, Lord. I know You are here with me," I murmured. "We made it through surgery. We made it through Friday! Thank You. Thank You."

Bett and Laura appeared in front of me. Words weren't needed. They rushed to either side of me, and we did our triple hug. Tears of joy flowed from all of us. The seriousness of this surgery, right on top of the others, had kept us stretched to the edge.

"I'm staying around," I said. Their heads nodded in agreement.

"I love you," Bett said.

"I love you, Daddy," Laura said.

"Thank You, Lord—for all of Your blessings and watchful care, my wonderful wife and daughter, and all those praying for me. Thank You for this new day and the extension of time You have provided. I will use it to Your glory. In Jesus' name, Amen."

Chapter 13

As fast as they had rushed me to the hospital, it seemed they wanted to get me out. My Friday surgery, according to my surgeon, would probably mean a Monday discharge. *As much as I wanted out of here, was I ready to be on my own? How would I manage even basic tasks such as washing myself or taking a shower? You need two legs for that. And what about getting in and out of places?*

"Good morning, Mr. Kasperski. How are you feeling? Did you sleep okay? Finish up your breakfast. You have physical therapy in half an hour," the nurse said.

"But I just had surgery yesterday, and it's Saturday," I said.

"Saturday doesn't matter here. Your doctor ordered therapy. An aide will be by to take you. Do you have any pain by the new incision?"

"No, not really."

"Then you're good to go," she said as she left the room.

Good to go. I hope I don't get a drill sergeant therapist to match her! Doesn't she know what I've been through? She should try to move around with one leg!

Reaching for the trapeze bar above the bed, I pulled myself up and turned to dangle my leg over the side of the bed. With slipper in place I stood, using the walker. *Uh-oh—the room is moving. Better sit back down. I need to give my body a little time to adjust before heading to the bathroom on my own.* I rang for the nurse. Thankfully, a different one came, and in time for me to get to the bathroom. As we came out, there was a man standing there with a wheelchair.

"Mr. Kasperski, time to go to physical therapy."

The nurse helped me put on a second gown in bathrobe fashion. (I need to keep my "respectability" at therapy.) Off we went.

"Hi, Michael—good to see you again."

"We'll start you with the basic cardio-vascular exercises and stretches today."

"Okay."

"Time to stand, Mr. K. We're going to have you stand for two minutes this time, okay? Let me know if you get too tired or feel dizzy. Wheels locked? Grab the walker and stand. Looking good, Mr. K. Do you feel okay?"

"Yes, I'm good. No dizziness."

"Good. Next, we'll have you walk to the bench with the blue mat. You can sit and rest there. Then we'll walk back. Sherry will follow you with the wheelchair in case you need to rest. Ready?"

"Okay," I said. Looking across the room, I realized that the bench looked pretty far away. *Here I go.*

"Place the walker out in front of you and hop up to it. Good. Again. Nice work, Mr. K. Take a rest."

He guided me to the bench. I was a little winded, but not too bad.

"Let's do it again, Mr. K., and then you're finished," Michael said.

"The last part sounds good."

Pulling myself up to the walker, I repeated the exercise. The last five feet drained me.

"Just a little farther . . ."

Going backward I felt a hand on my shoulder and hip.

"We've got you, Mr. K."

I landed in the wheelchair—a little hard, but safe.

"You did well. You'll be able to do this tomorrow, I'm sure," Michael said.

"Sunday?"

"Oh yes, we'll be here. See you then."

Getting close to my room, I heard the chatter of familiar voices. They turned around and the speaking stopped. Obviously they were startled by the sight of the missing limb.

"Hi, Mom. I'm okay. Hi, Greg. How are you, Kay? Was your trip all right?"

As they approached me, Mom, at eighty-one, led the pack and gave me the first bend-down hug.

"So good to see you, son. I was so worried."

Joyful tears flowed from both of us. My brother-in-law Greg grabbed my shoulder and hugged me too.

"Let me be part of the group hug," sister-in-law Kay interjected. "What a relief to see you, Stephen."

"Bett's updates pushed our imaginations out the window," Greg said.

"It's been a tough ten days, but I'm still here . . . well, most of me. Therapy will be a challenge. I just came from there."

"They started you on therapy already? You just had another surgery yesterday," Mom said.

"They don't let you rest around here. I have it again tomorrow. How long are you staying?" I asked.

"Until noon tomorrow. We got a room at the hotel where Bett is staying. Your mom will stay with her tonight. It's a great place, and reasonable for a patient's family members," Kay added.

"I wish I could be there with you. I can't imagine what this half-room is costing per day," I said.

"Thank goodness you got here in time and got the care you needed," Greg said.

"I know, and I'm *not* complaining. Prayer has gotten me this far. I'll be patient. I've even had some special visitors."

"Special visitors?" Mom asked.

"Do you remember the TV show, "Topper"?

With that another visitor arrived—my dear friend (more like a brother), Pastor Jim, from my former church two states away.

"When I heard all the noise, I knew I must be headed for the right place—a regular coffee klatch, Jersey style, was going on. The only thing missing, Stephen, is your cigarette," Jim said.

"Oh, I gave that up."

"You what?" the group responded in unison.

"Yes, they gave me the patch ten days ago, and so far I'm doing okay with it. But a good cup of coffee would be great," I said.

"You'll get your good cup of coffee on Monday," Bett said. "I've already got the place scoped out for you on the drive home, dear."

"Hi, everyone. Great to see all of you."

"Hi, Daddy," Laura chirped in a soft voice.

Hugs were exchanged around the room. What a wonderful feeling to see everyone in front of me. The warmth of family and dear friends—priceless!

A nurse popped in and reminded us about the maximum three-visitor rule.

"We'll take shifts," Bett answered on everyone's behalf.

Agreeable responses came from all corners of the room. And then, as quickly as they had assembled, several left.

"Good-bye, Daddy. We'll be down to see you soon. Hank is downstairs, ready to pick me up. It's about a seven-hour trip home, and the kids . . . well, I've been here a week so there's lots to do. I love you."

"Love you too, Laura. Glad you were able to be with me. You're the best."

Bett left and went to lunch with her brother Greg and his wife Kay. That left Mom and Pastor Jim with me. We were "visitor legal."

"It's so great to see you, Jim. Thanks for driving all this way," I said.

"Well, you might have left the area, but your 'northern' church family misses you and has been in constant prayer since Bett's first call. We've been praying for all of your family. Frankly, you put us in such a tizzy that I had to come. Now I can report this wonderful news of your recovery at tomorrow's service," Jim said.

"Thank you, Reverend, for praying for my son," Mom said.

"We've been praying for you too, Mrs. Kasperski," Jim said.

"For me?" she asked.

"Sure. Nothing is tougher than seeing your child in danger or suffering," Jim said.

"You're so right. We both needed to see he was all right. My prayers are answered," she said.

I lay humbly silent as I listened to both of them share their love and concern. It was indeed a special moment. *Thank You, Lord, for being here with all of us. Amen.*

Chapter 14

Sunday morning came, and I was on my way to therapy again. The equipment I needed was in use. Michael sat next to me, filling in a chart.

"You seem a bit like a fish out of water here, Michael. Have you always been a therapist?" I asked.

"Interesting that you should make that observation. No, these muscles—my "pumped up" build—came from years in construction as a laborer."

"Really? How did you end up here in this type of work?"

"About five years ago, a dear friend of mine came down with cancer. I had been out of the area on a job and didn't see her until the last two weeks of her life. I was devastated to see how frail she was. I asked her what I could do for her. She told me just to treat her like family and be with her. I said I would, and I stayed with her as much as possible in those last days.

"Two days after her funeral, I started training to be a physical therapist. Even though I may only see patients for a few days before they're discharged, I make the effort to treat them as my brother, sister, aunt, or uncle. I don't let them off easy, but I do try to reassure and guide them as if they were my family," Michael said.

"What a wonderful tribute to your friend, Michael. I do sense that your involvement is different than others. You're living up to your calling," I said.

"Thank you. Now let's get started, Mr. Kasperski."

"Please, call me Stephen."

"We're really not supposed to, but how about Brother Stephen?"

"Great."

"Okay, let's get walking, Brother Stephen."

I reached for the walker, lifted myself up, and gazed at that faraway blue bench. *I'll make it this time . . . and back.* Slowly hopping, I started "my walk." As I turned to sit on the bench, I felt people watching me. I looked behind me. There stood Kay, Greg, and Mom, motionless and silent. I sat down, and they rushed over to me.

"That was wonderful, Stephen," Kay announced.

"Unbelievable!" Greg said.

"A joy to see, son," Mom chimed in.

A reverent silence occurred as we relished the moment.

"God bless you, son."

Amen.

Chapter 15

Monday morning came. Bett checked out of the hotel in preparation for my departure. All of the other family members had left. Arrangements had been made for me to go to a rehabilitation center about fifteen miles from our home. While there, I would receive one to two weeks of therapy. The last place I wanted to go was another "facility." Yet, considering the multiple shocks my body had sustained, I knew I wasn't ready to be on my own.

The doctor came in for one final look at my stump and the other incisions from the aneurysm repair surgery. He told me that he was ordering a PICC line to be placed in my forearm. This thin tubing would be threaded through several blood vessels (arteries) to right near my heart. This traveling IV would be available for me to receive medicine as needed so I wouldn't have to be poked again and again. I wasn't too pleased with the idea, but since it was a condition of my release, I accepted this additional invasion of my body.

A special nurse arrived right after lunch to insert the tubing. It wasn't the best experience of my life, but an hour later I was getting dressed to leave. The pain from all my surgeries had been manageable, but with a hundred-mile trip ahead of me, I took my prescribed limit of meds.

"Hi, Stephen. Almost ready?" Bett asked.

"Yes, just help me with my socks . . . I mean, sock and shoe."

"What took so long with that nurse? I've been outside your room for almost an hour."

"They put some special access line in my arm. It goes directly to my heart."

"To your heart?"

"So I won't have to get poked all the time. I guess it's a good idea."

"It's almost three. They're expecting us at the rehab place by six. We were really lucky they had a bed for you. It's only fifteen miles from home. You're getting closer to being back where you belong. The social workers, both here and there, have been very helpful.

"I'll ask for an aide so we can get going. When they get you to the exit, I'll go get the car and come up front."

"Okay."

My first exposure in twelve days to the chilly outside air reminded me that it was now October. *Just get me in the car and out of here.* I was talking to the aide when Bett pulled up. I turned to look at the car.

"Where's the aide?" Bett asked.

I glanced behind me and was surprised to find he wasn't standing there. "He's . . . gone. Bring the chair to the car. I'll figure out how to get in."

Grabbing the arms of the wheelchair, I pushed myself into a standing position. I wiggled my remaining leg toward the car and reached for the door. Pivoting on my one foot, I got myself ready to sit in the car. I dropped myself down into the passenger seat. I pulled my leg into the car and let out a big sigh.

"Are you okay?" Bett asked.

"Yes, let's get going."

Bett put the rest of my belongings into the trunk, and we were off.

"Good-bye, Baltimore," I said.

We passed the baseball and football stadiums and got on the highway.

Grabbing Bett's forearm, I said, "What a relief it is to be heading home, at least to our home state. I want to see the house and go in before we head on to the rehabilitation center. It seems like I've been gone for months."

My unexpressed thoughts were, *I thank God, really thank God, that I am alive. Even though I don't want to go to another institution, I guess a week of gaining some strength and practicing walking is a good idea. At least there won't be any more surgeries. My body has been invaded enough.*

Chapter 16

"Helen will meet us at the house with the wheelchair her mother used. I just have to call her when we're about half an hour away," Bett said.

I just nodded because the strain was already getting to me. "How much longer?" I asked.

"At least another hour. Why don't you try to sleep, dear?"

The next thing I knew, I smelled good coffee.

"Here's your treat—a large, fresh-brewed decaf."

"Thanks, Bett. Life is good!"

As we entered our hometown, a rush of peace came over me. I was home. We pulled into the driveway, where we were greeted by a welcoming committee consisting of our neighbor Helen, standing by the wheelchair, and her son Roger.

"Welcome home, Stephen. Good to see you. You gave us quite a scare," said Helen, opening my door.

"I scared myself a few times, too. It's good to be here."

I turned myself toward the chair. "Are the wheels locked?"

"Let me check. Now they are," Helen answered.

I reached for the arms of the chair, stood up, anchored myself, and transferred to the chair.

"Roger can help you get in."

"Just tell me what to do," Roger responded.

A strapping athletic man in his mid-twenties, he was up to the task. As we chatted briefly in the driveway, another neighbor came over and gave me a hug.

"Good to have you back, Stephen. Bett's been keeping us informed, but there were a lot of worrisome updates," Shirley said as she welcomed me.

"It's great to be home," I replied.

Roger pushed me toward the garage and hit the apron with a jolt. "Ow!" I blurted out.

"Sorry, Stephen. I didn't think that was such a bump," Roger said.

Still grimacing, I just waved him to move toward the steps.

"How do you plan to get in, Stephen? You're looking quite pale. Maybe this isn't such a good idea," Bett said.

"Just give me a minute. I'll figure something out."

Since I was not a stranger to analyzing how to move safely, I pondered my options: three steps, perhaps four to get to the landing of the kitchen.

"Can you lift me in the chair going backwards, Roger?"

"I'm sure he can lift you and the chair, but are you up to those bounces?" Helen asked.

I was never one to give up, but right now exhaustion and pain made the decision for me. "Maybe you could just open the door to the house so at least I can see inside."

"Sure. Let me do that for you," Roger said.

As I watched him ascend those steps—taking two at a time—the impact of my inability to do the same hit me. Coming back with my drastic surgical changes meant that even getting into my own house would be a big challenge. Certainly that wasn't happening today. *How long would it take just to do that task?* With the door ajar I could see the counter and the table. I saw papers and even a blue plastic bag labeled "patient's belongings." I was here, and the house was here. There wouldn't be any view of the other rooms today. Letting out a big sigh, I uttered softly, "Take me to the rehab."

It was nearly 7:30 p.m. as we pulled up to the rehabilitation center. A nurse and an aide maneuvering a wheelchair approached the car.

"Mr. Kasperski?" the nurse asked.

"Yes."

"We've been waiting for you. Was your trip okay?"

"He made it," Bett answered. "It's been a very long day."

"We've got your room ready, right by the nurses' station so you can get whatever help you need."

Entering through the large double doors, we rolled to the hallway on the left. My senses reacted to my new environment.

It was hot and smelled like an "old people's home." *Where am I?* As I peered into the rooms we were passing, I could see mini-homes, complete with dressers full of personal possessions and TV's with the volume even too high for me. *Is this a rehab or a nursing home? Are they the same thing?*

We reached our stop.

The nurse yelled to the man in the room, "Hi, Danny. This is your roommate, Stephen."

There was no response from him. I could see his TV, which was showing the news. At least we'll have something to talk about. I hope he likes baseball, especially since the playoffs start tomorrow.

A curtain was drawn around my bed.

"Need help getting settled?" the aide asked.

"No, thank you. My wife will take good care of that."

Immediately, Bett began placing my belongings in the dresser.

"At least I can wear some real clothes in here," I said as she worked. "I'm really tired of my 'gown' wardrobe."

As I observed my new surroundings, the enormity of the task in front of me overwhelmed me. I needed to develop a whole new process of movement. I wasn't going to be confined to a bed. I didn't want to be limited in any way. I had always adapted to or even changed my environment to make it workable. It would be harder to do this time because my age and limb loss were big obstacles. *Time to get some rest and work on that plan tomorrow.*

Chapter 17

The clatter of trays awoke me as breakfast arrived. "Good morning, Mr. Kasperski. Did you sleep okay?" She placed my breakfast in front of me.

"I did pretty well, except you forgot to turn off my friend's TV," I said.

"Oh, Danny likes the TV on all the time. We never shut it off," the aide said.

Now, I do like to watch the news, but CNN 24/7? No way! Looks like I just got my first issue.

"We told your wife to bring a TV for you."

I must be in an older nursing home. Real places would have a TV.

"The social worker will be in, and then you'll have physical therapy. Someone will come to take you there."

Take me there. Two weeks ago I was walking. Covering my ears to block out the TV noise, I drifted back to sleep.

"Hi, Mr. Kasperski. I'm Annie, the social worker. I coordinate your care with your insurance carrier. They have approved ten days here to start. We'll see how you do and request an extension if necessary."

"I'm sure that will be long enough. No offense, but I'm determined to get out of here."

"That's a great attitude. I'm sure you will. I'll check on you in a couple of days."

The drape had been opened, and I could now see my roommate. His food tray lay untouched. He was lying in a half-fetal position, staring at the ceiling.

"Good morning, Danny Boy. Ready to eat?" With that, a nurse sat on the chair beside his bed and opened several containers. Placing a towel bib around his neck, she began to feed him. As she placed the spoon in his mouth, half of the liquid came back out. He made some noises, but they were not understandable words. I surmised that he had suffered a stroke and there was residual paralysis.

It makes you stop and think that the limb loss wasn't the worst thing that could happen. *I guess Danny, CNN, and I will work it out. Maybe we can watch the baseball game later.* I stopped and said a prayer for Danny and myself. *I guess we can help one another.*

Chapter 18

"Time for therapy, Mr. Kasperski. I'll get your chair," an aide said.

Wearing real clothes and being escorted to therapy, I was feeling pretty good about myself. *I'll do double what they ask.* Observing the rooms on this other wing, I noticed that they all seemed to be pretty much the same—a nursing home setting. Those who were dressed were lined up in the hall, close enough for conversation, but there wasn't any. I've visited enough friends in this setting, lined up as if they were at a bus stop, except the Greyhound isn't coming. It's a sad way to spend the remainder of life, but at least protected care is being provided.

"Good morning, Mr. Kasperski, I'm Jean, one of your therapists. How are you feeling? Any pain in your stump?"

"No, Stumpy and I are fine."

"Good. Let's get started. What types of exercises have you done since the surgery?"

"I've been walking with a walker."

"Great. We'll do some more of that, along with some upper body exercises, and then stairs."

"Stairs?"

"Yes, ever since Columbus landed here, we know our world isn't flat. You need to be able to get in and out of places safely. We'll show you how to do it. We won't let you fall."

She placed a walker, the old kind without wheels, in front of me.

"Now stand."

Going through the brake checklist in my head, I asked myself, *Wheels locked? Check.* I grabbed the sides of the walker and raised myself up. It felt good to be at normal height rather than chair level.

"Okay, Mr. Kasperski, try three steps. Terry will follow behind you with your chair. You can sit down when you need to."

First step/hop, fine; second step/hop, fine; third step, and I reached for the chair. Half falling backwards, I felt strong hands guiding my landing.

"You're okay, Mr. Kasperski. We're not going to let you fall," the voice behind me said.

"How do you feel?" Jean asked.

"A little light-headed. But I did more than that at the hospital."

"We're going to let you rest a bit. You've been through a lot. Your body needs to catch up on recent events."

With that, Bett appeared in front of me. "Are you okay? You look pale."

"I got light-headed after a couple of steps. How am I going to get around?" I took a deep, calming breath.

"Your body will bounce back. Give it some time to heal," Bett encouraged me.

"Yes, Mr. Kasperski, I know you will be a success story. Just give it some time without imposing any deadlines. We're done for this morning. See you later," Jean said.

"But we only did one thing."

"We did one important thing. We'll see you later. Come back at 2:00 p.m."

Bett began to wheel me back to the room.

"I can do it," I snapped, turning the chair around.

"Where are you going?" Bett asked.

"To the lobby and maybe to the parking lot," I retorted.

Wise as ever, Bett let me self-propel up the hallway. My arms and pride gave out about the same time. Gently grabbing my shoulder, I felt a squeeze of encouragement from Bett's hand.

"I'm sorry, dear," I said, my voice trembling.

"I know, Stephen. Let's get some fresh air. There are some benches out front. It's very comfortable outside for an October morning."

Chapter 19

"Hi, Stephen. How are you?"

"Good afternoon, Pastor. Good to see you."

"How are things going?"

"Okay, I guess. I'm not making great progress at therapy. I can do five step/hops before I need to rest."

"What do the therapists think about your progress?'

"They feel I am doing very well."

"Maybe your expectations are too high, considering all that you have been through. You were very sick when I saw you at the hospital. By the way, have you had any other 'visions' or extra visitors?"

"Not in a while, but I do feel another presence with me, especially when I become anxious."

"Well, I think we both know Who that is. The Great Comforter spends a lot of time with those in hospitals. I know that I feel a more intense Presence in critical situations. In fact, when I meet with a family encountering tough decisions or loss, I get nervous because I don't know what to say to them. But the words of comfort come to me immediately, without fail."

"I'm beginning to see that in others too, Pastor. I expect it from Bett with her deep-seated faith, but even the kids and staff around me have been an inspiration. I'm used to nurturing others, so it's humbling to be the recipient."

"Amen to that, Stephen."

"Amen, indeed."

"I feel like we've already been praying, but let's bow our heads together."

"Would you remember my roommate, Danny, in prayer?"

"Gracious God, we thank You for Your healing touch and Presence with Stephen. We thank You for his family and ask for strength for everyone as these life changes occur. Please comfort and sustain them. Be with Danny and his challenges. For the caregivers here, give them wisdom. We know You are the Great Physician. We trust in Your healing. In Jesus' name, Amen."

"Amen. Thank you, Pastor."

"The choir sends their love and misses that faithful bass voice."

"Tell them I'll be back soon."

Chapter 20

"Hello, Mr. Kasperski, I'm Dr. Harris. I check in on the residents here."

"I'm not really a 'resident' here—just here for therapy. Where's my doctor?"

"Your doctor is out of the country at the moment, and the covering doctor is not on our approved insurance list. I just need to check your wound and stitches. Are you having any pain?"

As the doctor pulled back the sheet, I asked, "What about my surgeon?"

"Are you going back to him for follow-up care?" Dr. Harris asked.

"Not if I don't have to. He is . . . his group is . . . eighty miles away. I meant my first surgeon at the hospital in town, Dr. Cato."

"I suggest you let me check on it, and then you can request, in writing, for Dr. Cato to come in. May I check your wound now?"

"Yes, okay. Ouch!"

"Sorry. It's a little puffy. The staples and stitches are not ready to come out just yet—maybe two or three days. Keep moving your stump, though, so it doesn't lock into a set position, and you can keep adequate circulation for healing.

"Has anyone talked to you yet about prosthesis?"

"No, not yet, but the therapists are setting up an appointment for the company representative to see me here."

"Good. Just remember that you need full healing, inside and out, before putting pressure on your remaining leg. Any questions?"

"No."

"Good luck to you, Mr. Kasperski. Keep fighting. Good-bye."

"Good-bye, Doctor."

Keep fighting? I didn't think I was fighting. Well, whatever . . .

"Hi, Mr. Kasperski. Remember me—Annie, your social worker?"

"Yes, what's up?"

"Well, your insurance needs an update, or they're kicking you out of here tomorrow. Was your doctor in?"

"No, my doctor is away, and the covering one can't visit me here for some reason. Dr. Harris saw me."

"Good. I'll check his notes. I'm going to request five additional days. Your therapy report indicates that you have quite a bit more to achieve. We can probably make the case for an extension. I'll let you know."

Five more days—not really to my liking. CNN is definitely getting on my nerves. At least Danny and I compromise and watch the ball games in the evening, and the staff lowers his TV volume around 11:00 p.m. My own TV is easier to see, and we only need the volume for one. If I could only get a good night's sleep, I think I could progress more at therapy.

Chapter 21

"Good morning. The doctor ordered some blood work," the nurse said.

"Take what you need—just leave me some."

"Good to hear you joking. We have so many patients who never say anything," she said.

"I noticed it's an older crowd."

"Oh yeah, but they're sweet—just old, mostly. All done. At least with your PICC line we don't have to poke you."

"When will that come out?" I asked.

"It's the doctor's call. They're waiting for you at therapy. Want them to come get you?"

"No, I'll get there myself. It gives me something to do."

"Go pump some iron, Mr. K."

"Yeah, right."

"Ready to try some stairs today? We'll do the short ones first."

"Okay. I need to accomplish certain things to get out of here. Let's go for it."

"Good. Come over here. We'll just do the three hops to the stairs first so you'll have enough energy left to do them."

"Okay."

"Wheels locked? Grab the walker and move to here."

Gripping the sides of the walker, I move forward—one, two, three. In front of me are the therapy steps, with rails on both sides.

"Now grab the railings. Concentrate on your foot and hop up. We're here. You're not going to fall."

I hop.

"Good. Again."

Hop.

"Good—now stand up straight and catch your breath. Take a minute. Coming down is a little trickier. Make sure your main weight stays toward your backside. Don't lean forward too much. We don't want your weight to carry you forward. Ready?"

Looking down—my foot feels frozen. I don't want to move. If I miss, I will take a hard fall. Down two steps to the hard vinyl floor. I begin to sweat.

"Mr. Kasperski, are you okay?"

In an instant three therapists are around me, one behind and two in front of me.

"Mr. Kasperski, we're going to get you back to your chair. Just concentrate on your foot. Can you do it now?"

I couldn't answer.

"Mr. Kasperski, can you turn around?"

Puzzled, I looked at her.

"If you can turn around, we can lower you into your chair. You don't need to hop. Can you turn around?"

My hands are sweaty, and I begin to feel very clammy. With that, I feel someone prying my hand off the railing and turning me. My other hand goes limp, and I let go of the railing. My knee is giving way.

Whoosh!

I hit something.

Bump.

Bump.

I hear someone say, "Check his pulse. Bend his head down."

Out.

Chapter 22

As I awoke, I saw Bett in front of me, without her usual smile.

"He's waking up," she called.

Someone reached for my wrist. "How are you feeling, Mr. Kasperski? Do you know where you are?" a voice said.

"Stephen, I'm right here."

"I see you, Bett. What happened?"

"You fainted during therapy."

"I what!?"

"You were doing the stairs, Mr. Kasperski, and it was probably too much, too soon. Are you feeling any pain?"

"No pain. I'm just very unsettled. My stomach is queasy."

"We'll get you some ginger ale. Your system needs to get stabilized. Did you eat before coming in?"

"Not much—just some cereal and that imitation milk," I said.

"Low blood sugar could have contributed to your light-headedness. Make sure you've eaten more food before your next session. See you tomorrow," the therapist said.

As Bett guided me back to the room, the enormity of my changed life struck me again. *If I can't do stairs, how will I get in and out of places? How will I get into my own home?*

Thank You, God, that I do have a good right leg. I can take care of the gas pedal and the brake. They're not going to take that freedom from me. The one thing I'm not giving up—driving!

Chapter 23

"Good news, Mr. Kasperski. You got your extension. You'll be our guest another five days," Annie, my social worker, informed me. "I heard about your problem at therapy. How has it been since then?"

"A little better and hopping farther each day."

"That's great. You have a good attitude and a higher-than-average helping of determination. During my years in this profession, I've discovered that those two things make for a successful transition to this modified lifestyle."

"Modified lifestyle?"

"You know, being an amputee."

Ouch! Having a "stump" for a leg and now being called—categorized—an "amputee" . . . another new identifying feature that I didn't choose.

"Are you okay, Mr. Kasperski? You look startled," Annie said.

"Okay, I guess. I'm just not used to my new title."

"Sorry. I should have been more sensitive to the newness of your condition."

"It was going to happen soon enough. It's not your fault."

"Hang in there, Mr. K. See you soon."

Straightening up I said to myself, *No pity party for me.* Meanwhile, my insides were aching. I wanted to go back in time, just three weeks ago, before all this happened. I wanted to be whole.

Chapter 24

October days were passing. I continued to make progress at therapy, standing longer, hopping farther, and even navigating the stairs a couple of times. Prayer and determination continued to propel me forward.

Bett and I were in the lobby when a noisy crew arrived.

"I told you to get better directions. You drive slower than I do," one said.

"Where's the bathroom? I gotta go," another said.

"I'm starving. They'd better have a snack bar here."

As they turned the corner, the cantankerous group saw me and went silent. Simultaneously, their eyes filled with tears. My brother Paul moved toward me and leaned down to give me a hug.

With voice cracking, he said, "Good to see you, Stephen."

"Glad you came, Paul," I said.

One by one they came over to greet Bett and me. The last one didn't move. I wheeled over. "Hi, Mom. I'm okay—really."

Not speaking, she pinched my cheeks as she always did. She grabbed the side of the chair to balance herself and hugged me tight. I broke the awkward silence.

"I love you, Mom."

"I love you too, son," she whispered.

"I'm feeling pretty good. Doing fine at therapy too. I'm walking more each day,"

"Walking?" my sister-in-law, Patty, asked.

Niece Joanie chimed in. "How do you do that?"

"I use a walker and hop. I'm getting pretty good at it. I hope to get to use crutches soon, but my big goal is to walk using a prosthesis."

"But you have no leg," Joanie blurted out.

"I have some leg. Wanna see?" They gasped. "Just kidding. It doesn't look that bad. Right, Bett?"

"No, it doesn't. The staples are ugly, but they'll be out soon. It looks like one of those large sausages you see hanging in the deli," Bett said.

"I'll never eat sausage again," Paul said.

"Seriously though, we have an appointment tomorrow with someone from the arm and leg company."

"Stephen!" mother said, almost scolding.

"At least you can joke about it. I don't think I could," Pat replied.

"It's the only way to go. I'm still here. The blood clot in the leg helped them find the aneurysm in my stomach. I've been given more time, and I plan to beat this too," I asserted.

"God bless you, Stephen. You are one good fighter, big brother. I love you," Paul said.

"It was good to see all of you. I'm really glad you came. The next visit will be at the house, I promise."

Chapter 25

" It's almost 3:30, dear. The representative from the prosthesis company should be here soon," Bett said.

"I'm glad that one of the two companies in our insurance plan visits rehabilitation centers. I'm anxious to get started with the fitting as soon as my wound heals," I said.

The sales representative came in the room and shook my hand. "Hi, I'm Ken from Embassy Prosthetics. Sorry that I'm late. You're my seventh appointment today. Here's my card."

"Do that many people need a prosthesis?"

"We sell many different products, but the prosthesis market is definitely on the rise with aging boomers, diabetics, and returning vets. I have lots of new clients, so I'm really busy."

"Good for you, I guess."

Without much fanfare he said, "Let's take a look at your stump. Okay?"

"Okay, but I do have some questions."

He put on gloves and pulled back the sheet. "Show me what movement you have. Okay, now the hip side. Again, front to back." He pulled off the gloves. "Not much to work with. Maybe we could fit you like a full hip disarticulation patient; but even so, keeping it on may be a problem, and your movement would be restricted. It's held on with a belt around your abdomen."

"But I've seen people running with a prostheses," I protested.

"Yes, we make those, but mostly for younger amputees from motorcycle accidents and for vets. They can cost from $50,000 to $100,000. The social worker told our office that you only have $10,000 coverage in your plan."

"What!?" I exclaimed.

"Yes, I think that's the number I heard," Bett said.

"You can always pay the difference or work out a payment plan. Any other questions? I do have two more appointments. Focus on healing. We'll be around when you're ready." The salesman departed.

Silence.

"I feel like we got the bum's rush," I said.

"I didn't care for his bedside manner. Even disturbing news can be presented more gently," Bett said as she reached for and patted my hand. "We'll make it, dear. The healing needs to happen first. The rest will come."

My usual positive take on things was rocked this time. Bouncing back was my style. I didn't like the options presented. *I wish this would all go away.* My surroundings spoke a different message. A trapeze bar over my bed helped me turn over and raise myself up. *Where's my wheelchair? Out in the hall. I can't even get to it. Lord, where are You?*

Chapter 26

I finally got a good night's sleep. I guess exhaustion played louder than CNN.

"Here's your breakfast, Mr. Kasperski. Two boxes of Cheerios, skim milk, and apple juice. Want some tea or coffee?"

"Only if you bring me the real coffee from the nurses' station."

"I'll see what I can do."

"Good morning, Mr. Kasperski. How are you feeling? Been to therapy yet today?" Annie, my social worker, asked.

"No, not yet. I just had some breakfast, but I don't have much appetite today."

"Well, be sure to get to therapy today because your insurance has denied you any more time with us."

"They feel I'm ready to be on my own? I don't even have a way to get into my house, except by hopping."

"I asked for another three days, and the answer was no. I see you face to face. Unfortunately, they . . . let me see how I can be politically correct with this. They see you as an escalating cost. Oops, that just slipped out."

"Has my doctor authorized this—to release me?"

"All I know, Mr. Kasperski, is that if you are here after midnight today, your insurance will not cover you. You'll be responsible for the bill."

"Guess I'm going home, ready or not."

"Going home?" Bett walked in. "Is he ready?"

"Statistically I'm ready; physically comes in second. I know you tried your best, Annie. Thank you for everything."

"You're welcome. Godspeed to both of you."

Bett grabbed my hand and we kissed good morning. "It'll be good to have you home. It's been almost four weeks now. The house is lonely without you."

"You know I want to be there. I'm just concerned about how I'll move around and do things for myself."

"There are no deadlines, dear. You'll do what you can do. We'll manage. We have good neighbors and friends at church. Many have offered to help. The kids will get here when they can. I'm not leaving your side."

"I know, dear. I love you."

"I love you too."

Time to say my farewells. In twenty minutes, I'll start with the physical and occupational therapists on duty. Things I want when I first get home: a good cup of coffee, real food, and no twenty-four hour TV. There's even a playoff game tonight. Bett and I will watch it together, like we always do. *Thank You, Lord, for carrying me and even giving me a wife who loves sports. I am blessed.*

Chapter 27

"Hey, Mr. Kasperski! I hear you're leaving us," the phlebotomist said as she entered the room with her tray of vials and needles.

"Yes, you only get to take my blood one more time."

"Okay by me. Give me a good report now. You feel a bit warm, Mr. Kasperski. How are you feeling today?"

"Not much appetite and a little chilled, but I figured the air conditioning was high. I know Danny likes it cold."

"I thought you felt warm at breakfast," Bett said.

The nurse touched the air conditioning unit. "It's not on. Let's check your temp. Have you been out of the room today?"

"No, I was just about to go to therapy. I just needed someone to bring my chair by the bed. They always move it when they bring the food tray."

Beep.

"103 degrees—you stay right there. The doctor is just a couple of rooms away."

"But that's not my doctor."

"We still have you here, so he's your doctor right now."

Minutes later my chill became a cold sweat. I reached for

the blanket to get warm. My hands were shaking. *What's going on here?*

The doctor entered. "How are you doing, sir? Any pain? Let's take a look at your leg."

He touched my leg, and . . .

"Ouch!"

"Does it hurt here, too?"

"Ouch!"

"We're going to start you on antibiotics through your PICC line. There are some brown crusty spots on your stump, and it's swollen and inflamed above that. Your wound could open at any time. Do not leave the room. You can go to the bathroom with a nurse or an aide guiding you. We don't want any rapid movements that might open this up. This appears to be a bodily response to an infection."

"But I'm going home today. My time's up here."

"Mr. Kasperski, post-surgical infections can be very serious. I do the doctoring, not the forms. You need attention—and right now."

I'm trembling all over now. "It's awfully cold in here."

"Nurse, bring more blankets. Call for an ambulance."

Bett's warm hand pressed into mine as she leaned over me. "I'll be right outside the door, dear. They're going to get you ready for transfer."

"Transfer?"

"To the hospital. It's in this same town," she said.

"Mrs. Kasperski, we really need you to step outside."

She kissed my forehead and pulled her hand away. I didn't want to release her, my anchor in this battle. Another blanket was placed over me. It didn't make much difference. I felt so cold. A nurse placed another fluid packet on my IV hook and made the connection. Two paramedics pulled a stretcher into the room. My stump began to throb. My bed sheets were pulled up around me.

"On three," said one.

"Careful of my leg . . . stump," I said.

"We've got you covered," I heard as I landed on the stretcher.

The IV bag hit my arm—so cold. The wheels began to turn. Ceiling tiles and lights were the only things in my view. Doors opened, and I saw the waiting paramedic truck. Another emergency ride. Lights flashed and sirens blared as we took off. *What's happening to me?*

Chapter 28

I sensed a familiar presence as I awoke. Then I heard Bett's voice, and I turned toward her.

"He's awake," she said.

I felt her kiss my cheek.

"What happened?"

Another voice chimed in. "Welcome back, Mr. Kasperski. Dr. Cato, here. How do you feel? Any pain?"

As I took inventory of my body, I sensed a dull pain in my left leg . . . stump. "Pain here." I pointed to my mini leg.

"I want to check it out, now that you're awake. If it hurts, tell me or raise your hand," Dr. Cato said.

As he put on gloves, I braced myself.

"Here? Here? Here?"

"Ouch!"

"Here?"

"Ouch!"

"Those brown spots that we've been watching have spread. We were hoping that they would dry up. If they get darker, that would be a serious concern. We need to arrest this infection. We'll use a combination of antibiotics through your PICC line and wet/dry dressing changes every four hours. We'll keep your temperature monitored and do blood work to see how you are responding to this treatment. Do you have any questions?"

"How did this happen?" Bett asked.

"Post-operative infections have become increasingly common. You were doing fine when we removed the staples, but this must have already been in your system."

"How long will I be here?"

"A few days—until your temperature drops and your blood count is stabilized. I'll check on you in the morning. The staff will reach me if needed. You've been through enough for today. Try to get some rest." With that, Dr. Cato turned and left the room.

"I was glad he was here when we got here. You can tell he cares," Bett said.

"But I was going home today."

"I know, dear, but home will have to wait a little longer. I'll stay and watch the ball game with you. One TV, one channel. Just you and me."

Our eyes met, and I signaled that was okay.

What did the doctor mean, "Get some rest"? Nurses barged in my room every few hours to change my dressing and take my blood. Breakfast arrived. Whoa, almost a real breakfast, except for the coffee.

"You got lucky, Mr. K. You got what the last patient ordered. Your diet plan will kick in for lunch," the aide said, noticing my expression. "Didn't I see you a few weeks ago on the fifth floor?"

"Yes, that was me."

"Good to have you back. You were on the way to emergency surgery last time I saw you."

"It's a long story."

"I don't need the details. You were really sick. We prayed for you, and you're still with us. Apparently, the Lord's not ready for you yet."

Chapter 29

"Good morning, Mr. Kasperski. How are you feeling?" Dr. Cato said.

"Better than yesterday. I'm still a bit hazy about everything that happened."

"Your body has endured many shocks. Your temperature is still 101 degrees. I think we need to bring in another doctor for your case."

"Another doctor? You were my first surgeon, and my regular doctor is coming home today from her trip. Why do I need another doctor?"

"I'm concerned about your new problem—the infection. I want to be sure we're doing everything to combat it."

"But I'm on antibiotics."

"Yes, and that may take care of it, but your healing may be reversing itself. I want to seek the opinion of an infectious disease specialist. Dr. Shafer works in the next building. He deals with that type of problem every day," Dr. Cato said.

"If you think that's necessary."

"Yes, I do."

"Okay. I just want to get out of here and stay out of here."

"I realize that. I'll arrange for him to come in. In the meantime we'll continue with the antibiotics and dressing changes every four hours."

10:00 a.m. *Where's Bett? Can't reach the phone, so I'll press the call button.*

"Yes, what do you need?" the aide rushed in.

"I can't reach the phone. The IV is in the way."

"Sorry about that. Is this better?"

"Yes, thank you. Can I get a trapeze to help me turn?"

"It hasn't been ordered, but I'll see what I can do."

"Thank you." I began dialing, but before I could finish, Bett walked in.

"Sorry I couldn't get here sooner, Stephen. Dan called. He's on his way and needed directions. He thought you would be at home."

"Me too."

"What's the matter? You seem troubled. More pain?" Bett asked.

"The pain is about the same. The doctor was in."

"And?"

"He wants to bring in another doctor."

"What for?"

"Because of the infection. He's calling in an 'infectious disease' doctor for his opinion."

"From Atlanta?"

"No, from right here."

"Maybe that's just standard procedure," she said.

"I've got the feeling he's more worried than he wants to say."

"Oh."

Just then Pastor Tom arrived. "Good morning, you two. I thought I would be seeing you at home today, Stephen. Sorry you're back in the hospital."

"Good morning, Pastor. Good timing."

"Good timing?"

"My surgeon wants to bring in another doctor, an infectious disease specialist," I said.

"They have procedures. Probably they're just being cautious. I see many people with trouble after surgery. How are you holding up, Bett?"

"Okay as long as he's making progress. Dan's on his way down for the weekend. We had hoped Stephen would be home, but at least he's near home," Bett said.

"Let us know what you need. The church family is anxious to help."

"Hi, everybody," Dan announced himself as he entered the room.

"Hi, Dan."

"Busy time here, I see," Dan said.

Two doctors appeared in the doorway.

"Good morning, Dr. Cato," Bett said.

"Good morning, everyone. This is Dr. Shafer. I've asked him to consult with me on your case," Dr. Cato introduced the man standing beside him.

"Good morning, Dr. Shafer. Good to meet you, I hope. This is my wife, Bett, Pastor Tom, and our son, Dan."

The new doctor nodded to everyone and approached me. "We need everyone to step out of the room. I had to fit you in between other appointments so we could see you today," Dr. Shafer said.

My family filed out.

"We'll be right out here, Dad," Dan said, escorting Bett to the hallway.

The doctors took up positions on either side of me, pulling the screen around me. They slipped on gloves, and Dr. Cato lifted the sheet, exposing my stump.

"These brown spots were receding a few days ago, but they have since increased, and discharge has started. We are doing wet to dry every four hours," Dr. Cato said.

No comment from the new man. He looked at the IV bags and then pressed on my stump.

"Ouch!"

"Sorry."

"Ouch!"

"Sorry."

As he backed up, he pulled his gloves off. He looked at Dr. Cato. "We need to triple up the antibiotics. Give it forty-eight hours, then do another assessment."

"Continue the wet/dry?" Dr. Cato asked.

"It can't hurt. I'll write the order for the new meds." Dr. Shafer turned on his heel and left.

"Hang in there, Mr. Kasperski," Dr. Cato said. He patted my shoulder and left.

Bett led the way, with Dan and our pastor following. "What did they say?" Bett asked.

"They're tripling my antibiotics and doing a reassessment in forty-eight hours. The new doctor is not Mr. Personality," I said.

"Did they say why they're doing all this?" Dan asked.

"Not to me," I said.

"Let's hold hands and pray," Pastor Tom began. "Gracious God, we know You're here with us, and especially with Stephen. We ask for Your strength to sustain Bett, Dan, and Stephen and for Your wisdom to be imparted to his medical team. We know You are the great Healer of hearts and bodies. Stand with us all. In Your precious Son's name, Amen."

"Thank you," I forced out with a quivering voice.

Chapter 30

The next two days passed very slowly, partly because my rest was interrupted every four hours for dressing changes, but more so due to my heightened anxiety. With all that I had been through—the surgeries, the setbacks, and the triumphs—it all boiled down to this: *I want to go home. Simple pleasures would suffice, such as being in my own room and bed with my wife nearby.* As I pondered those thoughts, I calmed down within.

"Mr. Kasperski? Mr. Kasperski? Your doctor will be here shortly. Do you need anything? Your wife is in our reception area. I asked her to wait until I changed your dressing. We don't need any extra germs near you," the nurse said. She worked swiftly and efficiently, removing the soiled bandage and replacing it.

"No, I'm okay," I answered, "still not much appetite."

"You've been drinking your supplement every day, right?"

"Yes, now that I have the chocolate one."

"Good. I'll get Mrs. Kasperski now."

"Thank you."

Soon I was looking at the face of my wife, the person I most wanted to see.

"The phone at home keeps ringing and ringing. Everyone wants to know how you're doing and when they can see you. Here's a new batch of cards. Almost a dozen came yesterday. We are blessed with so many good friends. Your equipment arrived this morning—a wheelchair, trapeze, and commode. The man who delivered it was very pleasant. How are you feeling, dear?"

"A little better today. The doctors should be here soon."

"Your color looks better. Let's hope we get a good report this time."

The doctors arrived. "Good that you are both here," Dr. Cato said. "Dr. Shafer has your results."

"Good morning. There's been some improvement in your numbers. The infection has diminished. We are about 40% there. I think we can continue with your antibiotic regimen four times a day for ten more days and take blood samples each week," Dr. Shafer said.

"Ten more days here?"

"No, it can be done through your PICC line. A nurse will show your wife how to do that. It can be done at home."

"Home?" I asked, my hope rising.

"Yes, home . . . with certain conditions. You can't leave the house. No visitors, except those who have already seen you. We need to keep your environment germ free. A nurse will show your wife how to administer the antibiotic," Dr. Shafer said.

"But I've never given an injection," Bett said.

"You don't actually give the medicine by injection. You hook up a ball with the medicine in it. The ball deflates in about half an hour, and then you disconnect the ball and flush the line. This needs to be done every six hours, so don't be late. The nurse who comes to draw the blood will show you how to do it."

"And the dressings?" Bett asked. Her voice revealed her growing anxiety.

"You will need to change the dressings. If the discharge changes color or odor or there is bleeding, call us immediately. Do you both understand?"

I nodded yes. Bett looked frightened and pale. Then I saw her gather her resolve.

"As long as they show me what to do, I'll do it," she answered confidently.

"Good," Dr. Cato said.

"This is our best plan of action for the next ten days. Call my office to schedule an appointment for the tenth day," Dr. Shafer said, and left.

"These superbugs often resist a single antibiotic. We hope the triple one will continue to defeat your infection. I'll put in the orders for your medicines. They should get to your house tomorrow. You can leave the hospital tomorrow afternoon. We'll get the nurse there about 5:00 p.m. We don't want you to miss any sequence of the drugs. Any questions?" Dr. Cato inquired.

"No, not now," I said.

"Okay, I'll see you tomorrow about noon before you're released."

"Thank you, Doctor. You've been wonderful," Bett said.

"You're welcome. Just work on getting this special guy better," Dr. Cato said.

"You can count on that. We're a team," Bett said.

Chapter 31

"I brought you some real coffee, dear, to celebrate your homecoming today," Bett said.

"I was worried that this day wasn't going to come. This old body has gotten pretty beaten up these past weeks," I said.

"There's a little late October chill in the air, but it should be just right by early afternoon."

"Any outside temperature is going to feel good to me."

"The nursing service already called. Someone will come to us between 5:00 and 7:00 p.m. The medicine will arrive just before that. I'm supposed to keep it refrigerated and take out one dose half an hour before use. It's a lot to remember, but we'll get into a routine. Oh, and one more thing," Bett said, slipping out into the hall. She pushed a new wheelchair into my room. "Here are your new wheels."

A reality check hit me. *Those were my new wheels . . . legs, really.* I wouldn't be walking into the house. I didn't know how I was going to manage it, but somehow I would be back home today, with the help of crutches, friends, and wheels. *Lord, give me strength!*

"Ready to go, Mr. Kasperski?" Dr. Cato said.

"Sure am," I replied.

"Just let me check your wound one more time. It looks about the same. Just remember to be careful not to hit it when you move about or transfer."

"I've already played the 'moves' out in my head. Mental preparedness has saved me from many a fall over the years. Even when I had my leg I needed to have a safe, alternate support lever because I never knew when my leg would give out."

"You're a remarkable man, Mr. Kasperski. I admire you and your wife."

"Thank you, Doctor," Bett said.

"I'll see you in my office next week. Keep changing the dressings. Call me if there are any other changes: a fever, pain, or significant discharge."

"Oh Doctor, when can I drive?"

"Drive? We'll see. Good luck."

Chapter 32

"What a beautiful afternoon! It's so good to be outside and going home. Look at the vibrant fall foliage. I don't think I've ever seen such vivid oranges and reds," I said.

"Sounds like you're looking through a new set of eyes, Stephen," Bett said.

"Maybe I am. I've been given an extension of my life."

Bett reached for my hand. "We have much to be thankful for," she said.

"Amen to that."

As we entered the driveway, I noticed that the lawn looked manicured. "Who cut the grass?"

"The neighbors have filled in for you. They've been great— checking in on me almost every day, too. It's hard to believe we've lived here a little more than a year. They are true neighbors."

A rush of emotion came over me, and I began to weep.

"What's wrong, Stephen. Are you in pain?"

"Not pain—joy," I forced out. "I'll be okay. Give me a minute."

"The counselors said this could happen. Remember, your body and psyche have been through many shocks. Crying and angry outbursts will happen."

"I'm just not used to losing control," I said.

"Maybe you're getting events in balance. You've had to fight to survive these weeks. I know it's drained me, but it has to be many times harder for you. Take a few deep breaths. You're home now."

"I can get out now."

"Okay, let me bring the chair around."

Locking the wheels, I pulled myself out of the car and transferred to the chair. "I can get over to the stairs. Just get the crutches there for me."

"No problem, dear. Take your time."

I locked the wheels, stood up on my leg, and faced the steps. *I need to make it up this time.* I grabbed the railing to steady myself. "Give me the crutch, dear." I steadied myself with the rail and crutch and leaned to the right. "Now get the wheelchair in place at the top of the stairs."

Bett hurriedly folded the chair and carried it up, opened it, and locked it in place facing me. "Is here okay?"

"Fine," I answered.

She came alongside me and then behind me.

"What are you doing?"

"I saw how the therapists braced themselves to grab you if you start to lose your balance."

"I don't plan to do that."

"Just in case."

"Okay."

Focusing on the steps, I led with the crutch on the missing leg side and hopped with the good leg.

"Good, dear. Three to go."

Crutch, hop.

Crutch, hop.

Last one. *Come on,* I told myself.

Crutch, hop.

Great! I'm inside.

I grabbed the side of the kitchen counter and dropped the crutch as I reached for the side arm of the chair, turning myself at the same time with a quarter turn of my foot. Going backward, I landed in the chair. It held my weight.

"Great job, Stephen!" Bett said.

Exhausted with this effort, I breathed a deflated sigh of agreement.

Safe at home.

"Give me a hug" Bett approached me, and my thoughts jumped back to our first days in this house only fourteen months ago. To simplify our lives, we had moved to a smaller home outside of the metropolitan area to work side by side and, eventually, retire. Those plans have changed in these past weeks.

My chair was gone from the table to make room for my wheelchair. *Too much to process right now.* Bett leaned down to hug me.

"You feel wonderful, dear. I know I'm shorter, but I'm still here."

"That's the most important thing."

We both squeezed each other with an even stronger hug.

"You have a couple of hours before the nurse comes. Maybe you should lie down."

"Yes, the trip and the steps have wiped me out."

Entering the bedroom, I observed my new accommodations: two large chrome bars held a triangular chain with a grab bar hanging below it. Hospital pads were on my side of the bed. I took this as a necessity, but a reality check at the same time. Life had changed for Bett and me. I was home but still a patient, needing treatment every four hours or really around the clock. I felt deflated for both of us. Dreams are not guaranteed, and ours seemed out of reach now.

I got into bed, and my eyes drifted around the room. Just seeing my stuff (my dresser, closet, and clothes on the rack) was comforting after five weeks away. While Bett waited by my side for me to get settled, I knew there was one thing I wanted to do before sleeping. We bowed our heads in prayer.

"Lord, thank You for bringing me home. Thank You for living with me every hour during this ordeal. Thank You for good doctors and other caring personnel, for the friends and family who have interrupted their lives to be at my side, and for Bett, my anchor and protector. Give us both the strength to see this through. In Jesus' name, Amen."

Smile.

Chapter 33

"Stephen, the nurse just called. She'll be here in fifteen minutes. It'll be better if we can be at the kitchen table. I'm sure there will be paperwork, and I need to see how to do the infusions."

Grabbing the trapeze bar, I turned toward the side of the bed. I dangled my leg and pulled the wheelchair closer. As I moved into the chair, the room started moving with me.

"Are you all right?"

"Just a little light-headed. Maybe I wasn't quite ready to be up. I feel okay now. The room stopped moving."

"You're still warm to the touch. Your temperature is probably elevated due to the infection. There's the doorbell." Bett touched my shoulder. "Stay put. I'll be right back."

I sat still and listened.

"Hi, Mrs. Kasperski. I'm Josie from the nursing services. Did the package arrive?"

"Yes, it's here," Bett said as she and Josie entered the bedroom.

"Hello, Mr. Kasperski. I'm Josie. How are you feeling?"

"Weak and tired, but very happy to be home."

"I'm sure you are. I read your case history. You've been through a lot. We'll get you set up and on the mend."

"Thank you. We're counting on you and the new drugs," Bett said.

"Let's get started. I'll need to draw your blood today, again in seventy-two hours, and then weekly. I'll overnight your blood to the lab, and the results will be electronically sent to your doctor. When's your next appointment with him?"

"In two weeks, unless there is a major change, high fever, or ruptured wound," I replied.

"Good. At least your PICC line saves me from having to poke you. Let me draw the sample," Josie said. "Where are the supplies?"

"Here, except for the medicine that is refrigerated. I took one ball out when you called, about half an hour ago," Bett said.

"Good, just the right timing. Where are the syringes?"

"Right here," Bett said.

"This is what you'll need to do, Mrs. Kasperski. I'll show you twice, so don't get too nervous."

"I don't have to give him any shots, do I?" Bett asked.

"No, it's all prepackaged. You just hook it up. But you do need to flush the line before and after the infusion with heparin."

We didn't need her to explain that heparin is a blood thinner. By that time, we had become pretty proficient with medical terms. Bett watched intently.

"First, you flush the line. Then you hook up the ball with the medicine. It takes half an hour to process. You disconnect the ball when it's deflated, and then you'll flush the line and recap the connection. Be sure to push the fluid in the syringe so there are no air bubbles. This procedure needs to be done every six hours, around the clock, for the next two weeks or longer, as the doctor orders. Any questions?"

"What about the air bubbles in the syringe?" Bett asked.

"Don't worry, it's not like the movies. A bubble is not going to hurt your husband. You'll get the hang of it quickly enough."

"As long as I don't have to give shots."

"You'll be fine. I'll see you in seventy-two hours. Here's my cell phone number if you have any questions."

Josie placed the red plastic "medical waste only" container on the counter. "Just keep this medical waste container away from any of your things. I'll use it on each visit."

Bett and I looked at each other. Our home was becoming a mini medical center. My wife looked pale and troubled.

"I saw what she did, too. We'll figure it out, dear," I said.

She nodded, but without much conviction.

- 8:00 p.m.—Dressing change.
- Midnight—Next infusion—that took an hour and a half. Bett was up at 11:30 to get the medicine out of the refrigerator. Midnight—hookup, 30 to 40 minutes for the infusion and then disconnect.
- 1:00 a.m.—Sleep.
- Repeat above infusion procedure at 5:30 to 7:00 a.m.
- 8:00 a.m.—Dressing change.

- 11:30 a.m.—Medicine out for noontime infusion.
- 4:00 p.m.—Dressing change.
- 5:30 p.m.—Medicine out for 6:00 p.m. infusion.
- 8:00 p.m.—Dressing change.
- 11:30 p.m.—Medicine out . . .

This is how our lives ran for the next two weeks. We were both zombies after a few days of this routine, never getting more than three or four hours of sleep at one time. The location of the PICC line made it difficult for me to do the infusion on my own. At particularly exhausting times, I remembered the lines of the marriage vows: "in sickness and in health; for better or for worse . . . ." We were certainly living those around the clock. I don't know what I would have done without Bett, but if the circumstances were reversed, I would have done the same for her.

Chapter 34

Overcast skies greeted us as we traveled to the office of the infectious disease specialist, Dr. Happy (my nickname for Dr. Shafer). I signed in. It looked like we would be there for a while. There were many patients ahead of us.

"Mr. Kasperski?" a nurse called.

"Yes," I answered.

"Please follow me."

Bett wheeled me into the room. Blood pressure taken: okay. Temperature taken: 99 degrees.

"Good afternoon. Your lab results show improvement, but the infection isn't gone. Your temperature is slightly elevated. I don't want to let this go much longer. Let me see your wound," the doctor said. "It's not entirely closed, still discharging, and warm to the touch. You can keep doing the dressing changes, and I will order two more weeks of antibiotics to be infused at home before the next step."

"What would that be?" I asked.

"Additional amputation to the hip bone. We need to clear your body of this infection."

I glanced at Bett. She had turned white. I think I turned red. My call on my body ran through my head.

"Any questions? Tell the front desk you need an appointment in two weeks." With no more comments, Dr. Shafer left to see his next patient.

We sat there, stunned. "I didn't like his suggestion. We need to beat this thing."

"We will," Bett quietly assured me, gripping my hand.

I don't think either one of us believed it at the moment. We needed to let this shock settle before reacting. It was a quiet ride home.

Chapter 35

"Hi, Josie," Bett greeted our visiting nurse. "Looks like you've got me for a couple more weeks. How are you, Mr. Kasperski?"

Actually, I was feeling a tad sassy that day. "No offense, but if I didn't have to see you, I would be better."

"I understand," Josie said, "but sometimes it takes more than one series to overcome an infection. You're getting a top combination of new antibiotics. Let me take your blood sample so I can get it to the lab."

And so it went—another two weeks of around-the-clock infusions and dressing changes.

That dark cloud of more surgery kept processing through my head. *More of my leg gone? How would I sit? How much more can my body and spirit take? Lord, please provide a way . . .*

We pulled into the handicapped parking spot outside Dr. Cato's office, and Bett brought the wheelchair around and guided me in.

"Doctor Cato will be in shortly to see you. Are you okay to get up on the examining table on your own?" the nurse asked.

"Yes, Bett is here. She can guide me."

At this point my strength was not very great; but by now, Bett and I acted like a team, and I accomplished the maneuver. We waited for the doctor.

"Good morning, Mr. Kasperski. How are you feeling?" Dr. Cato asked cheerfully.

"Okay. I don't have a lot of energy, but I think I'm adjusting," I answered.

"Let's see how things are progressing. Still doing the wet/dry dressings four times a day?"

I nodded yes.

With gloved hands, he began pressing on the wound. "Sensitive here?"

"No."

"Here?"

"Yes!" My body recoiled from pain.

"Sorry. Mr. Kasperski," he said pensively, "I want you to come to the hospital tomorrow morning, and I will re-clean, or debride, your wound. Even with your intensive antibiotic treatment, we have not conquered your infection. We need to be more aggressive. The procedure won't take long. You can go home after a couple of hours. Any questions?"

"Will this procedure take any more of my leg?"

"No, this is just a surface cleaning. I am concerned that these dark patches keep appearing and your wound is not fully closing. My nurse will give you the time and pre-operative instructions. Don't worry. See you tomorrow."

"Don't worry," I mumbled after he left the room. "He seems worried, well . . . concerned."

"Yes, he does," Bett responded, "but I know he'll do everything he can for you. He's a dedicated doctor."

I nodded. Bett wheeled me out of the exam room and over to the nurses' station.

"Nothing to eat after 10:00 p.m. Be at the hospital at 8:30 a.m.," she instructed, handing me a sheet of paper. *Here we go again.*

Chapter 36

The next morning, the staff at the out-patient section processed me quickly and readied me for surgery. On my gurney I was pushed to the OR. Dr. Cato, mask in place, greeted me.

"Good morning, Mr. Kasperski. We're ready for you."

I kept my eyes closed as the nurses worked efficiently to get me prepped, and soon another voice said, "Count backward from 20."

"20, 19, 18, 17 . . ."

"Want some juice, Mr. Kasperski? I know you must be hungry," a nurse said.

"Yes," I muttered.

"Do you know where you are?"

"Yes, at the hospital."

"Okay, that's good for now. Here's some juice. After that we'll give you some crackers. Your doctor should be around here soon. Who's waiting for you?"

"My wife, Bett," I whispered.

"Okay. I'll get her here for you."

"Thank you."

Half groggy, I felt a kiss on my cheek.

"Hi, dear. Has the doctor been here?" Bett asked.

"Not yet," I responded, and squeezed her warm hand holding mine.

Dr. Cato entered with a smile. "Mr. Kasperski, Mrs. Kasperski, it went well. We removed the dead scabby tissue and a little inflamed area too. That should help to erase the infection and speed healing. You can go home in an hour. Call me if there are any complications, but I do not expect any. Start your infusions again with the afternoon dose," Dr. Cato said. "Do you have any questions?"

"Will there be much pain?"

"No, more tenderness than pain. But I will order a twenty-four hour pain packet for you. Take two tablets every six hours. That should get you through any discomfort. Call my office tomorrow for a two-week follow-up appointment."

"Thank you."

He always makes you feel that things will be fine," I said a few minutes later to Bett.

"Yes, he does, and they will be," she said.

Chapter 37

We arrived home about one o'clock. I had advanced to hopping up backwards, using the new handicap railings put in by a friend. Even so, getting into the house sapped my final energy. I turned to Bett. "I need to lie down."

"Let me push you and help you get settled. I'll bring your lunch in here."

"Thank you, dear."

After downing soup and pain pills, I was out. No need for a Westerns channel to help me unwind. The cowboys could do without me today.

I woke up to a dark room as Bett turned on the little lamp near the bed.

"We're a little late on your infusion, so we need to get started. I'll do the dressing change after that," Bett said.

Still groggy, I just nodded.

"Don't you need to flush the line to get started?"

Repositioning my arm under the blanket, she said, "It's done, dear. I'm doing the disconnect procedure now. I'll be right back for the dressing change. Close your eyes, Stephen," Bett said as she returned. "I need to turn the ceiling light on."

"Go ahead. I'm awake."

As she pulled back the blankets, I heard her gasp.

"What is it?" I asked.

"There's a lot of blood here. All of the dressings are saturated—the pad underneath, too. How do you feel?"

I sat up to try to see what she was talking about but felt light-headed at the same time and rested back on the pillow. Bett hurriedly gathered more supplies.

"What are you doing?" I asked.

"I'm putting more dressings on top of these to absorb the blood."

"Aren't you going to change it?"

"I'm afraid to open up the bandage. That would just release the pressure, and I think we shouldn't do that. Let me get it reinforced, and then I'll call the nursing service. Let her change it. Just let me get the waterproof pad under you."

Things I didn't like were happening fast. Bett came back with phone in hand and described the situation to the nurse on the phone.

"Barbara is on call," Bett said to me after she had hung up. "She'll be here in fifteen minutes. She's been here before, but let me put the front lights on, and I'll be back."

I really hadn't moved but felt cold and warm at the same time. Bett looked at me and pulled the blankets back, exposing the area. She rushed to the bathroom and returned with more supplies.

"What is it?"

"The new dressings are soaked." She quickly wrapped a towel around my stump and secured a plastic bag over it.

The doorbell rang.

"Come in," Bett shouted.

Barbara appeared in the doorway and approached the bed. Bett quickly summarized what had just happened as Barbara put on gloves to examine me.

"Mr. Kasperski, you're losing a lot of blood. We need to get you to the hospital. I'm calling 911 for the ambulance. I'll also call Dr. Cato to tell him to meet us there." She dialed.

"You're not going to change the dressing?"

"No, what your wife has in place will hold us until we get there."

"I don't want to go to the hospital! I don't want any more surgery!" I could feel my body shaking.

"Cover him up!" the nurse exclaimed. "Stay with him. I'll wait by the door for the ambulance."

What's happening? The word *shock* flashed through my mind. I heard sirens, and two men burst into the room.

"I heard you're having a rough night, sir. We need to get you to the stretcher in the living room. Can you sit up? We'll help you to the wheelchair, and then transfer you."

Without a chance to object, I was being moved. As they lifted me, I could feel the cold wetness on my stump, and with that, the plastic bag and towel slipped off and dropped. All I saw was red. Someone quickly wrapped a pad on my stump and put me in the chair.

"Out of the way! Get another bag, stat!" They placed me on the stretcher, and we were out the front door.

"Bett! Where are you?"

"The neighbors are going to drive me to the hospital. I'll be right there."

The ambulance door slammed, and we were off. More sirens—but it was too surreal to comprehend.

Twenty, 19, 18 . . . out.

Chapter 38

Buckles released. "1, 2, lift."
I felt my body being moved.

"You're okay, sir. We just transferred you to the hospital stretcher," a voice said.

"Vitals?"

"BP 95/55 . . ."

I heard gloves snapping into place as a masked figure leaned over me.

"Mr. Kasperski, Dr. Cato here. Any pain?"

Trying to assess my condition, I uttered a weak "no" through the oxygen mask.

"Relax. I'm going to check your wound now."

"Ow!"

"Sorry," Dr. Cato said.

I braced myself as the probing continued.

"Found it."

Those were the last words I heard as I drifted out again.

As I opened my eyes, my left hand received a gentle squeeze.

"I'm here, Stephen," Bett said.

Thank goodness silently played in my head. "What happened?"

"The doctor said an artery ruptured from this morning's procedure. He'll be here soon to talk to you."

"What time is it?"

"A little before midnight."

"Mr. Kasperski, you continue to be a trooper," Dr. Cato remarked. "I want you to get fully stabilized before leaving the hospital. I've arranged for you to stay a day or two."

"I have to stay?"

"You lost a lot of blood, but I think we can wait on a transfusion as long as there's no more loss. Staying is a necessary precaution. I'll see you tomorrow afternoon. Get some rest. Good night."

While gazing at my dear wife, I witnessed the strain and exhaustion on her face. As much as I didn't want to be here, for her sake and mine, I guess twenty-four to forty-eight hours was manageable. *When will this nightmare ever cease?* "Go home, dear. I'm safe now. Thank you. I love you."

Chapter 39

Iawoke and took inventory of my situation: IV in the left hand, some kind of boot thing on my leg, and a covered tray in front of me.

"I heard you had a very rough night. How are you feeling?" a nurse asked.

"On a scale from 1-10?" I retorted.

"I guess if you can joke about it, you're okay."

"Actually, I'm trying to figure out how I am. There's no significant pain. What's the thing on my leg?"

"A compression boot. It's there to assist your circulation. It helps push the blood back up. We don't want any more issues with you."

I ate my hospital-fare breakfast and again dozed off.

My body clock woke me, and I rang for the nurse to disengage me so I could go to the bathroom. The boot was removed, and I transferred to the wheelchair. She pushed me, along with my IV pole. *What a way to live. I can't wait to get out of here!*

Bett was there when I came out. "Good morning, Stephen. Were you able to get some rest? How are you feeling?"

"Pretty good. I don't think I even need to be here. I can rest better at home. Did you sleep?"

"A little. Yesterday was a tough one."

That comment hit me. With all that's happened over the past months, Bett has never said how difficult these accruing episodes—or more accurately, crises—have been for her. *I need to remember and appreciate that my ups and downs affect my wife, along with me. I need to . . .*

"Stephen, are you okay? Your lips were moving, but no sound was coming out."

"I'm okay, just taking it all in. I just want us to go home together and get our lives back."

"We're together right now. Home will come soon enough, as soon as your strength returns."

I reached for her with my free arm, trying not to disturb the IV cord. She leaned over, and we hugged. In the tenderness of the moment, I could feel the bond of our love. Her fingertips on my shoulder, I squeezed her other hand and brought it to my lips. That simple touch covered it all. Our special union was intact. *Thank You, Lord. Through all of this, we've captured a new, deeper level of love.*

Chapter 40

"Good afternoon, Mr. Kasperski. How are you doing?" Dr. Cato asked.

"Good. I feel fine. Ready to get out of here."

"Your lab work shows a bit of a different story. I know you've been doing regular dressing changes, and the surgical procedure did remove the tainted scabs, but the infection is still not controlled. I want a vacuum system attached to your wound that will continuously pull out the infection. We are fortunate that, even though it's Saturday, a nurse specializing in this system is here today. I've ordered it for you. You'll need to be our guest for a couple more days while this begins. Then, I can order the portable unit, and it can be done at home."

"At home? How does this work? Will I get trained here?" Bett asked.

"No, a nurse will come in to change the dressing every other day. You will not do it. They'll show you what to do if the vacuum seal breaks. It's a wonderful healing tool. We need to get ahead of this infection. Any other questions?"

"Will this machine fix it?"

"It's our best avenue now. The nurse should be here soon. I'll see you tomorrow."

"I really thought we were over the hurdle—and now this other thing. I'm tired, Bett."

"I know you are. I'll be here. We'll beat this new challenge together."

"Mr. Kasperski, how are you doing? I'm here to set up the wound vacuum system. It's amazing how this system extracts infection. We create a vacuum by putting tape around your wound and the connecting tube. The machine continuously pulls at the tissue, and the secretions are collected in this reservoir. You'll get used to the sound of the pump. I see by your chart that your last pain medication was administered almost an hour ago. That should carry you through set-up time. The most you'll feel is some tenderness as I touch you.

"Mrs. Kasperski?"

"Yes?"

"You'll need to leave the room. We don't want any airborne germs to be present when his wound is uncovered," the nurse said.

"I understand. How long will you be?"

"Forty-five minutes, to be safe."

"Fine. I'll go to the coffee shop and come back, dear."

"Okay, see you then. Bring me a treat—some real coffee or something. Love you."

"Will do. Love you, too."

With mask and gloves in place, the nurse said, "I'm ready to get started, Mr. Kasperski. Any questions?"

"Okay, let's do it."

She started removing my bandage.

"Ouch!"

"Sorry. You have a large area to be uncovered and recovered. I'll move as quickly and gently as possible."

I tried to distract myself for the next thirty minutes or so, but this procedure was no picnic. *I only hope it does what's needed to rid me of this infection. Wonder when the next pain meds are due? Lord, I could use a little more help here.* I closed my eyes and turned away from the procedure. *Think quiet thoughts about comforting places . . . strolling on the boardwalk . . . oh yeah, strolling is a problem.*

"Mr. Kasperski, I'm all done. See, the noise isn't very loud. You'll get used to it. What are you feeling on your stump?"

"Just tightness and a slight pulling, no real pain."

"Good. That's exactly what we want."

Assessing the situation, I noticed that the tube from my wound was attached to the pumping mechanism affixed to the foot rail of the bed. So, I had an IV in one arm, a compression boot on my remaining leg, and this "wound vac" connected to my stump. That left one limb free—my left arm. *How will I move about?*

"Nurse, how long will this tape stay in place?"

"I'll be back in forty-eight hours to remove the tape, empty the reservoir, clean your wound, and apply a new connection and tape. Monday, about this time."

"How will I move about, turn in bed, and get to the bathroom?"

"Your movement will be limited to what you can do with the length of the tubing. This system isn't portable, so you'll need to stay in bed. I thought you were aware of that."

"No, I wasn't aware that I was being trapped in bed. I thought the 'portable version' was the smaller home model. I wouldn't have agreed to this . . . confinement."

"I'm sorry that wasn't explained to you. This extraction system has proved to be most effective in combating infection. Try to think of the bigger picture, Mr. Kasperski. All these steps are in place to help you get better."

"But I'm the one who's stuck!"

"I could hear your voice while I was coming up the hall. What's going on, dear?" Bett asked as she entered the room.

"I'm stuck. I'm trapped. I can't leave the bed even to go to the bathroom. Get me out of here! Give me back my dignity!"

Chapter 41

The next several hours tested my patience. *Try to think of the big picture, just as the nurse advised. Give the machine a chance to work.*

"Hi, there!" a voice said. As I turned, there was my brother-in-law, Brad, and sister-in-law, Ann.

"How are you doing?" Ann asked.

"Better than a few weeks ago, but I'm not there yet."

"Bett told us about the current complications, but we had already arranged the trip and wanted to see you," Brad said.

"I'm glad you got here. It's good to see you. I didn't expect to be back in the hospital."

"If you need to be here, this is where you should be. You can get immediate care," Ann said.

"I guess so. Getting bounced about in the ambulance was no joyride, though. Twice was more than enough. Now they've got me shackled to this bed."

"For how long?" Ann asked.

"At least until Monday when they change the wrap attached to this wound vacuum machine."

As I pointed to the machine, I noticed that they didn't look in that direction—at the missing leg side. *I guess anyone's first encounter with an amputation is tough to handle. I'll need to be aware of how others deal, or don't deal, with my changed body. Sad for all of us,* I thought as a large lump swelled in my throat.

"We're planning to take Bett out for a nice dinner tonight to give her a little break," my brother-in-law changed the subject abruptly. "She's called us many times in the past weeks. My sister puts up a good front, but you can sense the strain in her voice," Brad said.

"It'll be good for Bett to have some company. Wish I could go with you."

"When you're well," Ann comforted me. "We're glad we got to see you. We'll be seeing you soon, Stephen."

"Hang in there, buddy," Brad said, waving to me as they walked out.

The emptiness of the hospital room and the whole medical setting engulfed me after my company left. *I'm weary, Lord. Please send me some good news and healing. I don't think I can take much more.*

A vision of fishermen casting their nets filled my head, and I recalled the Scripture verse, "Casting all your care upon Him, for He cares for you." Calm replaced my weariness. *I can hang in a bit longer.*

Chapter 42

"Time to change your dressing, Mr. Kasperski," the nurse said. "How are you doing with the wound vac noise? Did it keep you awake?"

"Being stuck in the bed is the problem, not the noise."

"They should have the portable unit delivered to your home today or tomorrow. Then you'll have more mobility."

"Am I going home today?"

"That's your doctor's call. Dr. Cato should be here soon. When did you have your last dose of pain meds?"

"After breakfast, about three hours ago," I answered.

"Let's get this moving along right away. You will feel tenderness as the tape is removed. The reservoir is almost full. The machine is doing what it needs to do to remove infectious matter. Hold on now . . ."

"Ow!"

"Sorry."

"Ouch, that really hurts!"

"Not too much I can do about that. I'll work as fast and as gently as I can."

My tolerance for pain is better than average, but this procedure that involved pressing and pulling on my fresh wound challenged my endurance.

"I'm done," she said. She gathered up her materials and left.

I groaned in appreciation for the finished task. *This needs to happen three times a week? Hope this procedure works quickly. This is more pain than I had right after the amputation. And I was afraid of the expected pain. Funny, losing the leg hurt less than keeping the rest of the body whole. There must be some lesson in that, but I think I'll figure that one out later. Where's the doctor? I want to get out of here.*

"Did you see Dr. Cato out there?" I asked Bett.

"No, dear," she replied, walking into the room.

"I hate being hooked up to all this stuff. I'm calling the nurse. Where's that call button?"

"Yes, Mr. Kasperski? How can I help you?" the staff nurse asked as she walked briskly into my room.

"Is Dr. Cato here?"

"No, but he faithfully gets here sometime in the afternoon. Did you need something in particular?"

"I need to get out of here."

"How did the dressing change go?" Bett asked.

"Worse than expected. You know I can tolerate a lot of pain, but that was brutal."

"I know the wound vac nurse thought the machine was working well for you, even in this short time," the staff nurse said.

"Yeah, she did say that," I admitted.

"Good afternoon, Mr. and Mrs. Kasperski. How are you doing?" Dr. Cato asked.

"Good and not good," I answered.

"Let me see how the area looks. The wound vac is doing its job—extracting the infection."

"Ouch!"

"Sorry."

"Ouch!"

"That's it. No more handling today. But I need you on the machine until we know the portable one is in place. I'm afraid you need to be our guest at least one more day. We need to get ahead of the infection."

"Isn't there a portable one here?"

"No. This specialty item is too costly to just keep on hand. Hopefully your insurance carrier will allow it to be shipped or even delivered tomorrow. My staff will check on that early tomorrow. Until then, Mr. Kasperski, for your own well-being, we need to continue this course. Any questions?"

"No, I guess not. I'm disappointed. I'm really tired of hospitals."

"Hang in there, Mr. Kasperski. You too, Mrs. Kasperski."

"Thank you, Doctor, for everything," Bett said.

Chapter 43

"Be careful. Don't bounce me. I've got a lot of repair spots on this body," I said.

"Sorry, sir. I'm just trying to get you in the elevator before we have to wait ten minutes for the next one. With only two elevators in service right now, it's tough to do a 'speedy' checkout," the aide said.

"Hey, don't get me wrong. I'm happy to be leaving this place. There's my wife. See the green car? Bring me around to the driver's seat."

"The driver's seat?" the aide asked.

"Yes. I lost the left leg, not the right. I'm driving home."

"Are you sure you're up to driving?" Bett asked. "You've been in the hospital a few days."

"Yes, I'm up to it."

"Okay. I'll put the chair in the back seat. Just be careful when you transfer. You do have a lot of tape on your wound," Bett cautioned.

"I'll manage." I locked the wheels, lifted myself up, turned, and landed on the leather seat. One more turn and I had my hands on the steering wheel. I reached to lift my left leg in, as I had done for years because of the reduced strength, and realized what I had was already in the car. Habit had not caught up to reality.

"What's wrong, dear?" Bett asked.

"Nothing," I muttered. I put the key in the ignition, and we were off. I was happy and sad at the same time. Leaving the hospital was a good thing. Realizing that part of my body— damaged or not—was gone gave me profound feelings of loss. *Would I be able to navigate ever again on my own? Was my independence gone? What did I have left to offer my family, my wife?*

"Red light, dear."

"I see it." *Concentrate on driving*, I told myself, but my questions wanted answers.

Chapter 44

Finally settled at home, I heard some commotion in the living room.

"Hi, Dad. How are you doing?" Laura asked.

"Wow! This is a surprise—a good surprise."

"We didn't know if we would be able to come with the kids' schedules and all, but we juggled, and here we are."

With that, another head poked in the room . . .

"Hi, Grandpa," and Megan appeared.

"So good to see you and get some good hugs. Got anyone else hiding out there?"

"Well, actually Hank and Joey are making a few improvements for you."

"Such as?"

"They're installing some grab bars to make it safer for you getting in and out of the house."

"Really?"

"Bett told us how you were hopping backwards to get in—not a safe technique, Dad."

"Well, I need to get in and out."

"Of course, but at least the bars will give you something stable to hold on to."

"I appreciate it. I can hop fine, but I know that Bett worries."

"We all worry, Dad. No more big surprises needed. Just be careful."

"Guess what else, Grandpa?" Megan said.

"What?"

"We brought you a scooter."

"Yes, we know how you like to be outside and survey the 'estate,'" Laura chimed in.

"Ninety feet by one hundred and thirty feet is hardly an 'estate,' but I do like to check out the yard and all our plantings."

"Well, my patient is doing very well, getting about on his own, so he said he didn't need his scooter and that you could have it," Laura said.

"That's very generous of him. I know they cost thousands. I hadn't really thought about a scooter for outside, but it would be a good thing to have. Pushing my chair over any distance is a challenge. Thank you."

"No wheelies now, Grandpa."

"Why not?"

"Dad . . ."

"Okay, I'll think about behaving. Get me your patient's name and address so I can send him a thank you note."

"I will. Good to see you smiling, Dad. I know it's been a tough ride."

"Yes. But I've had support from so many directions—so many cards and calls. You know I'm a fighter."

"I know, Dad."

"How long can you stay?"

"Just until tomorrow."

"Good. There are some things I want to go over with you—you know, important issue things that require some private time."

"Serious things?"

"Yes, father/daughter things that I want you to know."

"You're making me anxious, Dad." Her voice quivered. "What are you saying?"

"I don't want to upset you and Megan, but there have been some close calls. We'll get to it soon."

"Okay, Dad. Soon."

"Let's have a group hug. Come here, my special beautiful girls. Let's go see that scooter. I think I'm ready for a ride."

"But the vacuum thing?"

"It's clumsy, but portable. It's not going to hold me back."

"Way to go, Grandpa."

Chapter 45

The nurse's visits continued to be our routine for the next several weeks. Bandage changes were less than pleasant, but the wound site was being managed by an R.N. This meant less work for Bett because she didn't have to change the bandages anymore. We got used to the noise of the pump, and I found two acceptable positions for sleeping with the connective tubing not in my way. A few times the seal broke, and a hissing sound started before the vacuum's alarm sounded. Bett managed to re-tape and keep the system in place until the nurse's next visit. Yet, the blood work showed only a minimal decrease in the infection.

"Be patient," the nurse advised, "these machines have turned things around in many cases." My patience was tested every day.

"Diane called, Stephen. She'll be here in half an hour to change the dressing. I'll bring your pain medicine in now," Bett said.

As much as I didn't want to keep taking these heavy doses of pain medication, it was still necessary to manage the site pain, as well as the phantom pain. For a long time after an amputation, the body reacts as if the body part is still there. To this day, the numbness where my ankle should be is still there, along with pain in the general area of my lower leg and foot. It didn't matter that the limb is missing. (The pills do take the pain away, however.) I've read that this phantom pain can go on for years, especially if you're older when the amputation occurs.

Today I had the "pleasure" associated with both pains—wound site and phantom. Pills were definitely needed before the dressing change.

"How are you doing, Mr. Kasperski? Pain level, from 1-10?" Diane asked.

"7," I replied.

"A little higher than last time." She pushed a thermometer toward my mouth.

Beep.

"100.8, also a little higher."

Bett stood at the end of the bed as Diane began to remove the dressings. Their chatter suddenly stopped as the wound was uncovered.

"When was your last visit to the doctor?"

"Two weeks ago, I think," I said.

"Yes, two weeks," Bett confirmed.

"This isn't looking good. Too much new discharge, and the color and odor are changing. Plus, your temperature is elevated. Your blood work will tell us more, but call your doctor and get in there for him to evaluate these changes."

Bett went quiet and just looked stunned. Each time there was a change in my condition, we went through it together. *What would this new hurdle be?* As difficult as the news and procedures had been over these months, we had learned to settle in and adapt to the new routine. The more flexible we were, the more quickly the repetition of care would become comforting because you knew what to expect.

Diane put the new wrap on, but even with all the pain meds having kicked in, my 7 went to an 8 and then 9. Something was happening fast, and it wasn't good. *Oh Lord, give me strength. Give me healing.* In between spasms, different thoughts and Scriptures ran through my head:

"When the going gets tough, the tough get going."

"Soar like an eagle."

"My cup runneth over."

"Surely goodness and mercy will follow me all the days of my life, and I will dwell in the house of the Lord forever."

"Nicole from Dr. Cato's office returned our call. He'll be back from his rounds in about an hour. She said to come right in. I'll get your sweats and shoe and help you get dressed," Bett said.

I had been dressing myself for the past couple of weeks, but today I put up no resistance. No matter what position I found, the throbbing pain in my stump continued. I reached for the trapeze and dangled my right leg over the side of the bed.

"Wait for me, Stephen. Let me be in front of you."

As Bett braced herself in front of me, I released the trapeze and began to fall forward.

"I've got you." Her voice got louder. "You're hot, Stephen. How are you feeling?"

"Light-headed and in pain."

"I'll get you fully dressed here so we can get you to the garage. I saw Dave's car across the street. I'll call him to help you to the car so there won't be any steps for you to attempt by yourself."

I nodded in agreement.

Bett drove to the doctor's office. We were both quiet on the way there with just the radio breaking the silence. She grabbed my hand at every traffic light. We arrived and I transferred to the wheelchair. She pushed me inside the doctor's office, which faced the hospital. I hope I'm not going there again.

A few minutes later, Nicole called us into an examining room. I stayed in the wheelchair because I didn't have any energy to get on an exam table today. Dr. Cato entered the room, along with another person.

"Good afternoon, Mr. and Mrs. Kasperski. This is Dr. Harbor, a friend of mine. With your permission, I would like his thoughts on your case. He was in the Army for a long time and worked with many amputees who had severe battle injuries and infections."

"Sounds like he could be of great help. Sure. It's nice to meet you," I said.

Both doctors put on gloves and approached me.

"We can examine you where you are. Please move as far forward as you can," Dr. Cato directed.

"Ouch! Where are you pressing?"

"Just above the tape line. I can feel your body's heat. What's your temp?"

"I'll take it right now," Nicole said.

Beep.

"101.2, Doctor."

"We've already alternated wet and dry dressings changes and used the wound vac. What would be your suggested next treatment, Dr. Harbor?" Dr. Cato asked.

"We've been very successful in treating stubborn wounds with HBO treatments, using a hyperbaric oxygen chamber. Do you have any wound care centers nearby?"

"I know there's one at Henson Memorial, about forty minutes from here. But I think another one just opened at Chester Regional, just twenty minutes away. I got a card inviting me to come to a physicians' reception. Check my desk for the card, Nicole."

"Will that cure this? What do you mean by a 'chamber'?" I asked.

"You have probably heard that deep-sea divers cannot come up too fast or they will get 'the bends,' a painful body reaction."

"Yes, I've heard of that."

"What they do to avoid 'the bends' involves putting the divers in a pure oxygen chamber, where they stay for one to two hours while their bodies adjust to surface atmospheric pressure. What has also been derived as a benefit from these chambers is that pure oxygen accelerates healing by helping the body to combat the infection," Dr. Harbor explained.

"Really? Does it hurt?"

"No, it doesn't hurt, but your body does have to adjust to the pressure changes. A nurse/technician monitors the pressure during your 'dive.' Basically, you just sit there or lie there through the whole thing."

"So this miracle healing can happen in two hours?" I asked.

"It would take a series of 'dives' for this procedure to work and turn the tide of this infection. The wound care group should have enough data and experience to know what you would require."

"Dr. Cato, I reached Henson Memorial," Nicole said. "They're booked for the next three weeks, but Chester Regional just opened Monday. They have an opening tomorrow for a consultation. I told them to hold it so I could speak with you and call back."

"What do you think, Mr. Kasperski?"

"What do you think, Doctor Cato?"

"I think that you need an additional avenue of treatment right away."

"What about the wound vacuum?" I asked.

"The vacuum system and antibiotics are still necessary," Dr. Cato indicated.

"I don't care what works as long as something does. Set up the appointment."

I looked at Bett. She nodded her agreement. A new day, new chapter begins tomorrow.

Chapter 46

At 11:00 a.m. on a blustery November day, we arrived at the hospital and looked for the Wound Care Center sign. We pulled into the parking lot near the front of this large hospital complex and asked the attendant, "Can you tell us where the Wound Care Center is?"

"It's right over there, just to the right of the main entrance. See the ramp?"

"Yes, we didn't see a sign," Bett said.

"It just opened. They don't have a sign up yet. You can park in this lot and walk over," the attendant said.

"My husband uses a wheelchair. Where is your handicapped parking?"

"In that case, go to the front of the building, and let him go in there. You come back to me, and I'll see that you get a parking place. It looks like all the handicapped spots are taken. On most days they're gone by 9:00 a.m., but we always keep a few protected spots. Will you be long?"

"We don't know. It's a consultation," Bett said.

"You take care of him. I'll cover the vehicle."

"Thank you so much," Bett said, then drove up to the door. "She was very nice—a good start to the day."

"Yeah," I muttered. My head was focused on the meeting. The last place I wanted to be was at another hospital.

Bett put on the flashers as she parked at the main entrance and then brought the chair around. As I transferred to the chair, a brisk gust of wind hit me and gave me a chill. I hoped it was only the weather conditions and not my infection escalating. *Lord, be with me and the doctor.*

As we entered the center, we could tell everything was brand new by the elegant matching décor of the chairs, tables, and the wall-mounted TV. I wheeled up to the check-in window. This was the first time that I had ever been to a doctor's office in which the reception window glass had two levels—one for patients standing, and one for those who could not. I mentally gave them ten points in the plus column for recognizing the reality of their clients.

"Good morning," the receptionist greeted me. "My name is Melissa. How may I help you?"

"Morning. I'm Stephen Kasperski. I have an eleven o'clock appointment."

"Yes. Since it's your first time here, we need some basic information. The input team will take the rest. Dr. Clark will be doing your evaluation. Please fill out these two forms—just what appears above the double line. We should be ready for you in a few minutes."

"She seemed quite nice, and the place is so clean and new. I feel good about this, Stephen," Bett approved.

I gave a half-hearted nod of agreement, but she was right. *So far, so good.*

"Good morning. I'm Theo, center manager. Please come back here to examination Room 3."

We settled in, and a gray-haired gentleman of slight build entered the room.

"Good morning, I'm Dr. Clark. I read your history. You've had a tough few months. Let's see if we can get that turned around for you."

"That would be wonderful," Bett inserted. "Everything has been so exhausting, and he has courageously met each challenge."

"Yes, good news and a cure are welcome," I said.

"Let's take a look at that wound. When's the nurse's next visit for the wound vacuum change?" Dr. Clark asked.

"This afternoon, about four o'clock," I answered.

"Good. We can give you a little break from the machine and not lose any significant extraction time. Holly is our staff nurse. She'll be gentler than I am. I've been a heart surgeon for years. My patients are always sleeping when I work on them. I guess I'm gentle too because they never complain."

I began to laugh, and that felt very good. Humor and an exceptional background—I was getting good vibes today.

"You do have a very active infection, Mr. Kasperski. Has it been like this since your amputation two months ago?" Dr. Clark inquired.

"At first the wound closed up fine, but at the rehab it got inflamed. I ended up back in the hospital because of the infection. It just doesn't end."

"You're a prime candidate for oxygen chamber treatment. I recommend that we start with ten sessions and evaluate you from there."

"Ten sessions? How quickly can that happen? How often are the treatments?"

"Treatments are two hours a day, five days a week, for two weeks."

"You think that will cure this infection?" I asked.

"I can't guarantee that right now, but similar cases have had extraordinary success. You can speak with Melissa up front about scheduling and other paperwork. Then Theo can show you the chamber and explain how it works as soon as the current patient is finished. See you soon. We'll take good care of you."

"What do you think, Stephen?" Bett asked, once we were back in reception.

"The only time we have an opening is at 8:30 a.m., Mr. Kasperski. Who is your insurance carrier?" Melissa asked.

"I have the card right here," Bett offered.

"We need to get the treatments approved. I'll fax them today. Hopefully, they'll respond right away, and we can get you started on Monday. I'll call you as soon as I hear back."

"Thank you," I said.

"Mr. and Mrs. Kasperski, you can see the chamber now. Follow me," Theo invited.

Bett wheeled me past the dimly lit reception area into a large room. I saw a TV monitor hanging on the back wall, a computer station, and right in the middle of the room—a horizontal clear tube. There was a large door half open that had many dials and a big handle. The chamber looked like a torpedo tube. *I need to be in* that *for two hours?* My fear antennae surfaced. *I really don't want to do this. Is there any other way?*

Then a surprising calm came over me. I read the name of the chamber manufacturer—Sechrist. I broke it down into two syllables: See-Christ. I got my answer. Help was here, and I was in the right place.

Chapter 47

"Stephen, the Wound Care Center is on the phone. Pick up.
"Hello, this is Stephen."

"Good morning, Mr. Kasperski. This is Melissa at the Wound Care Center. I've faxed the request for your HBO (Hyperbaric Oxygen Treatments) to your insurance carrier. They denied your treatment."

"What!? Can they do that? I need this, or . . ."

"Sometimes we have to ask more than once," Melissa said. "Dr. Clark put a detailed description of your situation to move things along. Maybe you can call and find your patient case manager. We can start your treatment, but you would have to be financially responsible. The treatments are about $1,000 each," Melissa said.

"I can't afford that for ten treatments. Who should I call?"

"Call your insurance company, give them your file number, and ask for your case manager. I still have you on the schedule for Monday at 8:30 a.m. Let me know by four o'clock tomorrow if you'll be coming. Good luck, Mr. Kasperski. Hang in there."

"What happened, Stephen? You look very distraught. Are you in pain?" Bett asked.

"Yes, insurance pain!" I barked. "They denied the chamber treatment."

"What? But the infection . . ."

"I know—not good news, and not many options. Maybe this is it for me, Bett. I'm tired and not winning this battle."

"Did she have any other suggestions?"

"Yes, we could speak to my patient case manager or something like that. I don't know that I'm up to that," I answered.

"Let me do it, Stephen. You're too sick to handle this now. I'll call for you."

"Okay, I guess. I'm just so tired of this battle."

"I'll get you some soup and your pain meds. Diane is due here soon for your dressing change. Then I'll get the patient manager on the phone. We're going to get a 'yes,' even if I need to call them ten times. I'm a Jersey girl, remember?"

"Okay, Bett. Do your thing. Thank you. I love you."

"Love you too, dear. The team goes on."

Chapter 48

Bett is driving. It's seven o'clock on Monday morning, and we're on our way to my first treatment.

"What did you say to them, Bett?"

"I was nice, then firm—but still nice. You can catch more flies with honey than vinegar. I wasn't about to lose this battle. The case manager went to the higher-ups, and whatever she said, it worked. She's a nurse herself, so she understood all the steps of your treatment. She has a military background, so she's witnessed the positive effects of the oxygen treatments coupled with the wound vacuum. She's another angel the Lord has put in our path."

"Amen to that."

"How are you feeling, dear?"

"Tired. I didn't sleep much because I was so anxious about this new treatment. I know it doesn't hurt, but staying in that tube for two hours . . . . At least my pain level is manageable."

"Here's our turn. I'll drop you off at the front again. It's too cold for you to be going in from the parking lot. Someone else will need the handicapped space anyway."

"Good morning, Mr. Kasperski. Good job with the insurance company. All ten 'dives' were approved."

"My wife called."

"Well, whatever you did, Mrs. Kasperski, it worked."

"I did have some heavenly assistance," Bett said.

"You're our first patient for today. The nurse is waiting for you. Go right back there to her station."

"Good morning, Mr. and Mrs. Kasperski. I'm Holly. I met you briefly last week."

"Yes, good to see you," I said.

"I need to take some vitals before we get you started. I'll take your blood sugar readings before and after your procedure. We want the level to be about 160-200 before we start and no lower than 80 before we'll release you. The pure oxygen lowers your blood sugar and accelerates your metabolism. 175, good. Just where we want it," Holly said.

"I'm surprised I'm that high. I took my medicine."

"An infection impacts your blood sugar. Now, you didn't use any deodorant, aftershave, or hairspray?"

"No, I'm clean. I read your instructions."

"Good. We want your body to receive all the benefit it can from the pure oxygen. There's a changing room and lavatory over there. Please remove all your clothes and put on the drape provided. Use the lavatory and come back. Your wife can accompany you."

"It's a little complicated, but Holly knows what she's doing," said Bett.

Bett wheeled me to the changing room. There weren't any bars to lean on, so I used the locker as my base to hang on to. Reentering the room, I transferred from my chair to the waiting stretcher. A white sheet and a blanket covered me.

"Okay, Mr. Kasperski, we need to get you wired up. We'll monitor your heart rate and blood pressure while you're in the chamber. I'll disconnect your wound vacuum tubing and reattach it after your treatment. Here's your 'buddy' to take on your 'dive.'" She handed me a urinal.

If I was wired up and lying down, how could I use my 'buddy'? I guess there's a way if necessary. Good thing I only had a small coffee.

"What kind of movies do you like?"

"Movies?"

"We have a DVD player with sound piped in for you to watch during your 'dive.'"

"Okay? Got any Westerns?"

"How about Clint Eastwood?"

"Good."

"You guessed right on that choice, Holly," Bett said.

"We're just about ready. Here's what will happen. When you go into the chamber, I'll lock the door behind you. The pressure will be the same as out here. It will take about fifteen minutes to get you to the required level for the best oxygen exposure. I'll be right here the whole time, speaking to you on the telephone. Your wife can sit right alongside the chamber. After ninety minutes, we'll bring you up in pressure, and that will take ten to fifteen minutes. We're only going to do thirty minutes today for your first time. If you have any issues, changes, or severe anxiety, we'll terminate the 'dive.' It will still take time to bring you up. Do you understand what I have said?"

"Yes. What about the movie?"

"Yes, Mr. Kasperski, I'll start that right away. Kiss the missus. We're ready."

I kissed Bett and gave her a "thumbs up." I even made a motion with my hands like I was swimming. *Now the real test begins.*

The door closed behind my head, and I heard the lock seal. It was just me in the clear tube in this dimly lit room. Monitors were registering me, with Holly in front of me. Bett was seated in a folding chair to my left. *Help me, Lord. Heal me, Lord. There's Clint. Okay for now*

"You did well, Mr. Kasperski. How do you feel?"

"I feel okay, but it was confining."

"I know. When I went for training from the chamber manufacturer, each trainee had to do a real 'dive.' Did you get the prescription for anxiety pills filled that Dr. Clark gave you?"

"Yes, I took one before I came in today. It said I could take up to three."

"Tomorrow will be the same procedure, but longer. If you're feeling anxious, take two pills tomorrow about half an hour before your 'dive.' Remember, no deodorant, aftershave, or hairspray."

"I understand about the first two because they could block your pores from receiving the oxygen, but why not hairspray?"

"Do you use hairspray?"

"Oh yes, he does every day. He's very fussy about his hairstyling," Bett said.

"Well, don't use any of it. Your hair could ignite and catch fire in the oxygen," Holly said.

"Well, you got my attention," I said.

"I'll hide the can. Igniting is *not* an option."

They chuckled. I had a rather unpleasant visual roll through my head.

Chapter 49

It's 7:15 on Tuesday morning, and we're leaving for the Wound Care Center. Getting me into the car, with the tubing and wound vacuum attached—and making sure the pumping was *not* interrupted—was its own challenge. Then Bett loaded the wheelchair into the back seat. This morning we had dense fog to deal with, in addition to my needs. *The chamber* is on my mind.

"Are you okay, Stephen? We're about twenty minutes from the center. You'd better take your pill."

"Good morning, Mr. and Mrs. Kasperski," Melissa greeted us. "Go right back. Holly is ready for you."

"Good morning," Holly welcomed us. "How are you two?"

"Okay."

"Go back and get ready. Use the lavatory, and we can get you prepared. I'll get Clint set up so you can see the rest of the movie."

I repeated the procedure of the day before with Bett assisting me.

"Sugar level good. No deodorant, aftershave, or hairspray, correct?"

"Correct."

"Let's get you wired up and your wound vacuum disconnected. And here's your 'buddy.' I even put your initials on it for you."

"Thank you," I muttered. *My own personalized 'buddy.' What a life.*

The stretcher loaded me into the chamber. The door behind me locked. Holly was in front of me, and Bett was seated in a chair alongside the chamber. *"Dive" two, here we go.*

"I'm going to start your descent, Mr. Kasperski. Can you hear me okay?"

"Yes."

"Focus on the screen, Mr. Kasperski. Here's where we left your movie yesterday."

I looked up. There was Clint doing what I used to do—being confident, free, and walking. I closed my eyes. *Are You there, Lord?*

Chapter 50

"Good morning, Holly. You seem especially chipper today," I observed.

"I'm rejoicing because one of my patients 'graduated' yesterday. It's surely an answer to prayer," Holly said.

"Graduated?" Bett asked.

"Yes. She was our first patient at this new center. She travels sixty miles from the Virginia shore to come for treatments. Her open sores resisted all other methods. The chamber and prayer have turned things around. I pray for all of my patients."

"You do?" I commented.

"Sure do. I pray for you while you're getting ready and then when you're preparing to leave. There's always time to check in with Him while I'm waiting for you."

"How thoughtful of you, Holly," Bett said.

"It's part of my 'healing' training. Let's get you hooked up, Mr. K. Do you like "Paladin"? Your skin feels clammy. Are you okay today?"

"I didn't sleep much last night. Maybe I'll doze during the treatment."

"That will be fine. Your wife and I will be right here alongside you. Remember, just speak to me or wave if you have any issues."

I nodded. Foot first, I entered the chamber. The door locked behind me. (I hate that sound.) The movie and the descent began. *Close your eyes, Stephen. Wake up when it's over.* I could feel the gradual change in my surroundings; it felt colder and tighter in here today.

"You're all the way down, Mr. K. I have back-to-back "Paladin" shows for you. They only come in black and white. Enjoy," Holly's voice quietly echoed.

I wonder if there's Thursday night football? Where is that remote? I reached in the arm of the chair. Not there. Let me try the other side. Not there. Bett, do you have the remote? There it is, on the coffee table. I'll have to get up for it. Pushing the lever on the recliner, I stood up. Bam! What was that? Bam! What's hitting me?

"Mr. Kasperski! Are you all right?" a voice questioned.

"What are you doing, Stephen?" I heard Bett's muffled voice at a distance.

Alarms went off.

What are these wires?

Where am I?

"Get me out of here!" I shouted.

Then I saw three faces around me: Bett, a nurse, and a man.

"Lay back, Mr. Kasperski," the man said.

"Calm down, calm down!" the nurse commanded.

"Listen to them," Bett added, her voice full of intense concern.

"What's going on here? I just want to watch the game. What's all the fuss? Leave me alone. It's my house," I yelled, pulling at the wires.

Another person appeared. "Mr. Kasperski, it's Dr. Clark. Can you hear me?"

"Yes."

"You're at the Wound Care Center. You're in the chamber. Do you know where you are? Please, relax. Calm down."

Center? Chamber?

"You need to relax so we can bring you up. Do you know where you are?" the other man stated.

Four faces stared at me. *Where am I?*

Bett stepped closer to me and put her hand near mine. Instinctively, I reached for her hand but hit a hard, clear wall instead. Then it hit me: *I'm in the chamber.*

"Get me out. Get me out! Unlock the door," I pleaded.

"We'll get you out, but it will take fifteen minutes. See the clock on the wall? It's 9:45. We'll have you out by 10:00," Holly said reassuringly.

"Watch the clock.

"Focus on the clock.

"Relax. I'm beginning your ascent. It's 9:47. Watch the clock, Mr. K."

"Ten minutes to go, dear. Be calm. I love you," Bett affirmed.

"Three minutes to go," Holly said.

I heard the door lock release and felt the stretcher being pulled out.

I could see the ceiling and feel the cool air of the room on my head and my shoulders. Bett pressed on my arm and then took my hand.

We connected.

I'm okay.

I took a deep breath. *Lord, if I've got to do this, You've got to help me!*

Chapter 51

My exhausting Monday through Friday 'dive' schedule continued: up at 5:45 a.m., leave by 7:15 a.m., and travel thirty miles to the Wound Care Center with all my traveling equipment in tow. Arrive, prepare, "dive" two hours, and then return home. My energy level plummeted more each day.

"We're almost there, dear. Time to take your pill," Bett reminded me.

I reached for the bottle in the car's cup holder, and took two pills today. Energy down, anxiety up.

"Are you okay, Stephen?"

"Anxious. I thought I needed some extra help today. What number 'dive' is this?"

"Eight," she replied.

"Oh, I thought it was nine."

"No, it's Wednesday. This is number eight."

"Bett, don't sell the car."

Silence.

"Did you hear me? Don't sell the car. If things don't work out, someone in the family can use it, or you can trade in both cars and get a new one."

Her hands gripping the steering wheel, she put on the directional signal, pulled over, and stopped. She began trembling and covered her face with her hands.

"Bett?"

She turned to me, her face red and tears dripping down into her lap. "You love this car."

"Yes, but I'm just trying to provide."

"You're not giving up, Stephen. I won't let you!" Her voice cracked as the volume increased.

Reaching for her hand, we shared a special moment of marital commitment—the two of us were one. My rock, my anchor, was sinking. I had to keep us both afloat right now.

"It'll be okay, Bett. God will carry both of us. Forget about the car. We'll be all right."

She gave me a weak nod.

"Are you okay to drive? We need to get to the center."

"In a minute," she said softly. "Just . . . just give me a minute."

I saw her swallow back her tears, and slowly we pulled out.

Chapter 52

"Good morning, Mr. and Mrs. Kasperski. Dr. Clark wants to speak to you before your treatment. You can wait in Room 3," Melissa directed.

Bett and I shared a concerned look as we headed toward Room 3. Very soon, the doctor arrived.

"Good morning. How are you two doing?"

"You tell me, Doctor," I said.

"Things could be better. Your lab results show the infection level since you started the hyperbaric oxygen treatments to be about the same. Have you had any more pain at the wound site?"

"No. I'm very tired, though. The schedule to get here every day is exhausting."

"Understood. When is the nurse coming to change the wound vac dressing?"

"This afternoon," Bett said.

"I would like to do three things: examine your wound now, proceed with your treatment, and then send you over to the radiology department to have a scan of your stump. It won't take long. I can have them wheel you over on the stretcher and bring you back. That's one big benefit of having the Wound Care Center attached to the hospital. Do you agree to this procedure?"

"What time is Diane coming today to change my dressing, Bett?"

"Not until three o'clock."

"Okay, Doctor."

"Good, I'll set it up. Let's get your wound vacuum disconnected and take a look. You can have a break from this machine for a few hours."

He reached for exam gloves, put on a mask, and began to remove the wrap.

"Ouch!"

"Sorry."

"He usually has pain meds before this procedure," Bett explained.

"I'll be gentler," he said as he continued to cut away the wrap.

I gripped the sides of the exam table to steady myself through the pain.

"Mr. Kasperski? Mr. Kasperski? Nurse!"

I woke up and felt a mask on my face and heard a monitor beeping. Something squeezed my upper arm and then released it. An IV stand stood near me. A figure wearing a surgical mask came over to me.

"How are you doing, Mr. Kasperski? Do you know where you are?"

"Where's my wife?"

"We'll get her. She's right outside in the waiting room. Do you know where you are?"

I took a mental inventory of my surroundings and attachments. "At a hospital?"

"Yes, at the Wound Care Center. I am Theo, the center manager. We met a couple of weeks ago. You fainted when the doctor was removing your bandage. On a scale of 1-10, with 10 being the highest, how is your pain level?"

Again I took inventory. *It's bearable.* "5."

"Good. It should lessen. We put some pain meds in your IV. You were thrashing quite a bit."

I noticed the wound vacuum on the tray next to me shut off. *Not attached.*

"The doctor will be with you shortly. In the meantime, I'll send your wife in," Theo said, and left.

Bett entered the room. "Stephen, how are you feeling?" She leaned over, touched my shoulder, and kissed my forehead.

"Okay."

"Your color is better," she said.

"What happened?"

"Dr. Clark was removing your bandage. You started trembling and fainted."

"The pain was intense."

Dr. Clark arrived. "Mr. Kasperski, how are you doing?" he asked.

"Okay."

"Good. We have cancelled your HBO treatment for today, but I would still like you to have the scan done. Can you manage that? You just need to lie down."

"What's the purpose of the scan again?"

"I'm concerned about the intensity of your infection. I thought we would have had improved readings in your blood work. However, the antibiotics you are taking, the wound vacuum, and the oxygen chamber treatments have not suppressed the infection. This scan of your wound area will show if the infection is present not just in the tissue, but in the bone."

"In the bone?" Bett gasped.

I fell silent. My life jumped back fifty years when I had a form of bone cancer. Amputation had been considered then. Thankfully, radiation treatment arrested the cancer. Had it come back?

"The test is not painful. You just have to lie still while the images are taken. Can you do that today? I'll get the results as soon as possible. I should have them when you come in tomorrow. I have other appointments scheduled in the hospital, but I'll come over and speak with you. May we proceed?"

"I've already delayed the nurse's visit until 5:00 p.m. You'll be her last stop," Bett said.

As they both stared at me, waiting on my response, many thoughts and repeat challenges played in my head. *Three surgeries, three hospitals stays, serious home nursing episodes, the hyperbaric chamber treatments, doctors, doctors, doctors . . . go forward or accept my fate? What should I do?*

Part of me wanted to give up. *Hadn't I been bashed around enough?*

Bett squeezed my hand. Something deep in my spirit rose up and said, *Fight!* Bypassing logic, in an almost "Twilight Zone" experience, I heard myself say, "Okay, let's do it."

"The radiology team is ready for you," Dr. Clark confirmed to me. As he exited I heard him say, "He's ready."

Two aides stepped in and loaded the IV bag on my chest, disconnected the other equipment, and I was ready to go. Bett was still by my side.

Theo met us at the door of the exam room. "After radiology, they'll bring you back here. You can leave your coats and the wound vac here. This is your room while you are with us. We'll watch out for you," he said.

Good news, bad news. I guess my "frequent flyer miles" have entitled me to my own room, number three—the good news. The bad news—my room is at a Wound Care Center.

Chapter 53

"We've been waiting for you, Mr. Kasperski. Dr. Clark made it clear that we're to take care of you right away and be gentle," the technician said.

I nodded.

"Dr. Clark seems very thorough and attentive," Bett commented.

"He's top-shelf all the way. You know, before he does surgery he checks the cleanliness of the OR. Nothing but perfection will satisfy him. Let's get you started. We need to make you radioactive for the images. You may feel a little warmth as this enters your bloodstream. We can do the photos after twenty minutes."

I felt a mild burn as the fluid entered my body through the IV. I closed my eyes, and even in the cold lab room, I sensed a larger warmth holding me, like a big warm blanket just out of the dryer. *Thank You, Lord. I know You're here.*

"We're ready to proceed. Are you okay, Mr. Kasperski?" the technician asked.

"I'm fine. Let's go."

"I'm just going to position your limb so we can get the best images. Hold still."

"Ouch!"

"Okay?"

"Ouch!"

"Sorry."

Click, click, and click.

"Done. Good job."

Just get me home.

Chapter 54

"Taking one or two pills today, dear? We're about twenty minutes from the center."

"Two." I didn't mean to be abrupt with Bett. I'm just worn out.

"Your room is ready, Mr. Kasperski," Theo said.

Bett wheeled me over to Room 3.

"Good morning. Did you sleep all right last night?" Dr. Clark asked.

"Fair. With the machine attached and thumping, it's annoying," I said.

"I have your results from the scan. We found a 'hot spot' on the bone in your stump. And the bone itself is mottled and moth-eaten in appearance. Were there any photos taken of your leg before the amputation?"

"I don't know. Everything happened so fast. I was in two hospitals with the blood clot before the amputation. It would be in the records. Do you remember, Bett?"

"Not really. We were told about treatment options. I am not sure about all the tests. It was all very stressful."

"Of course. I really wanted it as a frame of reference because of the bone's 'moth-eaten' appearance. That could be from your radiation years ago. Our bigger problem is the 'hot spot.' That is the signal of concentrated infection. I want to schedule fifteen additional chamber treatments."

"Fifteen more?" Bett and I chorused.

"Yes. I don't think five or ten will do it, and you just have today and tomorrow approved. If you agree, we'll provide an update for your insurance carrier and make the request," Dr. Clark stated.

"Any other choices?" I asked.

"This is the better choice. We need to rid you of the infection. The higher the numbers go, the more dangerous for you. The only other choice is to remove the remaining bone."

"Just the bone?"

"No, the remaining part of your leg—your stump—up to your hip bone."

Bett gasped and turned away. I felt nauseous and helpless. I had so little of my leg left. *How would I sit and function? Forget driving. This is too much. I am too much of a burden.*

Silence.

"Remember, we do have the oxygen treatments to attempt to turn this around. We have not reached the other option yet. I will do your summary today with these new findings and get them to your carrier. Okay?"

Silence.

Bett turned around, eyes puffy and face red. She grabbed my arm. "You can do it, Stephen. Please, do it."

Our eyes met—

"Okay . . . *for you.*"

Chapter 55

" **T**GIF—Thank Goodness It's Friday—last treatment of the week. Even I'm getting tired of Westerns."

"Now, that's hard to believe. I think you would be happy if the batteries died in the remote, 'saddled' on your Western channel," Bett joked.

"Saddled. Cute, Bett."

"Well, you do love them."

"Yes, the good guys always win. Works for me."

"We're here. You took your pills?"

"Yes, twenty minutes ago."

"Good. There's a big chill in the air today. It feels like snow. I'll drop you off up front. Bonnie always saves a place for me."

"Bonnie?"

"She's in charge of the parking lot. She asks about you and is praying for us."

"All prayers are welcome. Thank her for me."

"I will. See you in a few minutes."

Theo held the door open for me, and I turned the wheelchair around. It's easier to gain momentum up the slight incline going backwards. My right leg gives me leverage, and it's also my brake.

"Good morning. Go right back. Holly is waiting for you," Theo directed me.

"Good morning, Mr. Kasperski," Holly smiled as she greeted me. "It's Friday—your last treatment for the week. I found an old black-and-white Western for you at my library. It's ninety minutes, so it will cover almost all the time you're in the chamber. I can sing to you after that."

"Are you in the choir?"

"No, they didn't want me. I don't know why. I can read music, and I sing loud," Holly said.

"We had a pastor like that. We used to turn off his microphone during the hymns."

"Your blood sugar level is good. No aftershave, no deodorant, no hairspray?"

"None of the above. I'm non-combustible."

"Good. Here comes the missus. Go get ready. It's a good day for a 'dive.'"

It was a routine day at the Wound Care Center. All went well for me. With my 'dive' completed, it was time to leave. *Hooray! I really need the two-day break. Bett does, too. Getting us both up, out, and here by 8:15 a.m. is a big challenge.*

We were leaving when Theo intercepted us. "We just heard from your insurance company. They have denied you any further treatments. We'll ask again after today's blood work hits the system, but unless you can promise to pay $1,000 per treatment, we have to suspend any further treatments. I'm sorry."

"Do they know about the bone scan, the 'hot spot'?" I asked.

"Yes, that was outlined in detail in Dr. Clark's report."

"How can they just decline when these treatments are so critical?" Bett asked.

"Off the record, they look at the bottom line. We don't always agree with their decisions," Theo said.

"All these years we have paid for this insurance and *not* used it. I'm going to call the case manager. Maybe she can help," Bett stormed.

I could sense Bett's anxiety, but that "Jersey girl" trait was showing, too. I certainly was not up for the fight, so I was glad my "rock" was back in the game.

Chapter 56

It was a quiet ride home. We had just finished lunch when the doorbell rang. I didn't even turn around to see who it was.

"Hi, Pastor Tom. It's good, very good, to see you," Bett said.

"Hi, Stephen. How's it going?" Tom asked. "Still doing your 'dives'?"

I didn't answer.

"He's completed ten 'dives,' but the doctor requested fifteen more," Bett said, her lips beginning to quiver.

"And?"

"They denied us. I guess we've cost them enough. Our card must be maxed out."

"Sorry to hear this. Were the 'dives' helping?"

"A bit, but the infection has not been contained. There is concern that it's in the bone," Bett said.

"There must be a review or appeal process. Do you have a case manager you can speak to?"

"Yes, I plan to contact her as soon as Stephen is settled for his afternoon rest."

Reaching for our hands, Tom said, "Let's have a prayer together. Gracious God, please be with Stephen and Bett as they face this new challenge. We know You are the Great

Physician and able to heal our hearts and bodies. We ask for your continued healing for Stephen. Give the doctors wisdom to find new avenues of treatment. As Bett cares for Stephen, sustain her. We love You, Lord, and pray for all things in Jesus' name, Amen.

"Keep me posted. You have my cell number."

"On our speed dial," I said.

"Thank you for coming, Pastor, at just the right time," Bett added.

"I was on my way to see some members at the nursing home, but I got the feeling that I ought to stop here first. I know to listen to that Voice. Now, it's on to the nursing home. I'll touch base with you later."

Bett supervised my transfer from the chair to the bed.

"I can do it. Go do what you need to do." It was a mild protest. I was very tired. I didn't even turn the TV on. The bedroom door opened on its own. I guess Bett hadn't fully closed it. I was just beginning to doze off and could hear Bett explaining the new challenge—the denial of further treatment. Not that I really wanted to do so many more treatments, but the other options were so drastic and dangerous. My idle, mental drifting was interrupted. I heard Bett sobbing out the words,

"Please do something. We're losing him!"

Chapter 57

The next day passed quietly, and my pain level was manageable. Many "what if" thoughts played in my head.

What if I need more surgery?

What if the infection spreads?

What if my options have ended?

Then, I remembered a sales meeting several years back with the boss's breakdown of the letters YAHOO: "You Always Have Other Options." Don't give in, don't give up—just alter your path.

"Bett! Bett!"

"Are you all right? Are you in pain?" Bett rushed into the room.

"No, I'm in hope," I responded.

"In hope?"

"Yes, I'm in hope, and I have hope for the future—our future. I want to go to church to worship and see my friends. Let's go tomorrow."

"But the doctor didn't want you exposed to too many people because of infection concerns."

"Well, I already have one of those. I know this is the right thing to do—what I am supposed to do."

"Are you sure you have the strength for this? Especially the first time back? It will be quite emotional," Bett cautioned.

"I'll go just before the service and sit up front and leave right afterward. I want to be with my church family. I know you miss going, too."

"Of course, I miss being there. Even though we've lived here only fifteen months, we have made some good friends. They've been so supportive with cards, calls, meals, and prayers."

"So, it's settled. We're going!" I exclaimed.

The rest of the day flew by. Joyful thoughts filled my head. *We're doing something normal, not medical. Thank You, Lord—we'll be at Your house tomorrow.*

It was Sunday. Getting dressed in regular clothes felt good, instead of wearing sweats for therapy.

"I want to drive, Bett."

"Really? Okay!"

I got my wheelchair positioned alongside the car, clicked open the lock, opened the door, and prepared to transfer to the driver's seat. I stood, pivoted, and put my butt in first—always, always the safest way to go. Even with two legs, I employed this procedure; it eliminated the hazard of being off balance or falling by the car. Butt in—good. I reached to lift my left leg, and oh, not there. I took it in stride. I was in the car. It felt strange and comfortable at the same time.

"I'll put the wound vac here," Bett said as she placed it in my former foot spot.

Another reality check. *Change. So be it.*

Bett placed the chair in the back seat and sat beside me in the passenger seat. With seat belts in place, we started off for church. What comfort this basic activity provided. Life was where it should be—where it had been.

We reached the church parking lot. Bett smiled at me, and I reached for her hand. A quick clasp, and I kissed her hand. Before I could get the door, there was a knock on the window.

"Welcome home, Stephen. It's so good to see you. Are you singing with the choir?" Bruce asked.

"Not today, but soon."

Friend after friend came over with warm greetings and hugs for me and Bett. They helped me into the sanctuary. As the congregation saw me being wheeled in, they rose and started clapping. Tears of joy flooded my eyes and theirs. *It's so good to be in the house of the Lord. Amen.*

Chapter 58

Monday morning came, and my body clock was still set for an early morning departure, but with no need to go anywhere. I tried to extend the euphoria of Sunday, but reality knocked very hard. Things had gone well after the amputation. I was hopping with a walker, managing the therapy room steps with a crutch. Now with this infection, I had less and less energy. *Where will I go from here?*

I closed my eyes, more to block out my circumstances than to sleep. In front of me was a large room with many empty chairs. I reached for my trapeze bar above the bed to help me move, when I realized it was gone. *How am I going to move? Who would help me? Where am I?* Suddenly four figures were in front of me, all dressed in black. I recognized them as members of my Rotary Club. *How nice of them to visit.*

"Hi, Carol, Barbara, Denise, and Linda. Thanks for coming," I said.

They didn't respond. They came closer, and I heard their words.

"He looks good."

"What a struggle he had."

"Months of therapy."

"He looks at peace."

I reached for the trapeze bar again, grabbed it this time, and jolted myself awake. Peering around the room, I noticed my familiar surroundings were in place—dresser, lamps, TV, and wheelchair. *Where had I just been?*

Get a grip, Stephen. No more dreams like that. My reality isn't so bad. I'm still fighting the good fight.

Chapter 59

"Stephen! Stephen, turn the water off so you can hear me!" Bett said.

"I was just getting ready to shave. What is it?"

"The Wound Care Center called. They got approval for all the treatments. You can go today at noon. Holly will work through her lunch to get you in today. We need to leave as soon as you're dressed."

"Wow! That was quick. Wonder what happened to get their decision reversed?"

"Don't know. Your angels must have stepped in again. You said you were 'in hope.' Maybe your 'in hope' is bringing you to full health.

"You're going to make it, Stephen—changed, but richer than ever. You have a wonderful testimony to tell others with all that you have been through, lifted up again and again by God."

"You're right, Bett. When I woke up with that terrible pain in my leg months ago, I thought that would be it. I took two aspirin and prayed, calling on God to bring me through that day. With all the pain, disappointment, and struggles these past several months, we've never been alone. We've had each other.

When I was weak, you were strong. When you were shaky, I was able to reach down and gather strength. God has been so good to us and always with us. So many angels along the way—doctors, nurses, and friends who cut the lawn without asking. We've been sustained and lifted up. I know there are better things and ministry to come. I'm not disabled, I'm redirected. I just need to do things differently than others do. Someday I hope to get out of the chair, but if not, God has given me a new way to travel and witness. I'm ready to go for my next 'dive' treatment. I want to drive there today. Chamber, here I come!"

"You want to drive the whole thirty miles?" Bett asked.

"Don't worry, Bett. I've got GPS—God-Powered Strength. We'll be fine."

Trust in the Lord with all your heart,
And lean not on your own understanding;
In all your ways acknowledge Him,
And He shall direct your paths.
Proverbs 3:5-6 (NKJV)

Epilogue

Stephen continued his "dives," completing forty-six before the medical team was satisfied that the infection had been sufficiently contained. The wound vacuum system continued for another month beyond the chamber treatments. He remained on a moderate dosage of antibiotics for an additional two years. Stephen needed no further surgery on the remaining leg.

Stephen had three attempts for being fitted for an artificial limb—a prosthesis. The very short stump, plus other residual damage to the tendons in his hands from propelling the chair, forestalled that success. Six years later he still experiences bouts of phantom pain—common for amputees. He feels the limb—foot, ankle, and calf—and pain in all three places.

Stephen uses a manual wheelchair most of the time. He uses a power chair on days when he is more challenged by weakness. He uses a scooter to move around the yard. He does ride the power mower and cuts the lawn as strength permits.

Stephen is active in church, where he sings in the choir and serves as an elder. He is a Rotarian and serves on the board of directors for his club. He speaks at schools and to those facing personal challenges about his experience. An inspiration to others, he reminds many that he isn't disabled; he just does things differently. I am always nearby, checking on my adventuresome partner.

As you might expect, Stephen still drives.

Bett Kasperski

Meet the Author

Betty Lewis Kasperski is an educator, business leader, inspirational speaker, and writer. Coming from a family of educators and business owners, she feels comfortable in a variety of settings, including public speaking. She holds a master's degree from Syracuse University and resides in Sussex County, Delaware, with her husband, Stephen. Betty will soon complete preparation for her third career as a certified lay minister.

Meet Stephen Kasperski.

Even as a young boy, ordinary days came infrequently to Stephen. Affectionately called "the little old man," family members knew he carried adult burdens.

Betty Lewis Kasperski

Students from the Destiny Christian School (Reliance, Delaware) enjoyed learning about Mr. Stephen Kasperski's experiences and positive approach to life's challenges.

Glossary

Amputation — removal of a limb or any appendage of the body

Amputee — a person with one or more amputated limbs

AAA also known as Triple A — Aneurysm of the abdominal aorta

Aneurysm — weakness of the wall of an artery, dilated artery that may rupture

Debride or Debridement — the surgical removal of dead tissue from a wound surface

Heparin — synthetic preparation used to keep blood from clotting also aids in clearing a line

Hyperbaric Oxygen — oxygen at greater than 1 atmosphere

Hyperbaric Oxygen Chamber — a sealed, enclosed setting where oxygen level is raised, treatment is used to accelerate healing and combat infection, treatment referred to as "dives"

ICU — Intensive Care Unit in a hospital, critical care patients receive constant monitoring

Infusion — the introduction of a fluid into a vessel

OR — Operating Room-place where surgery is performed in a hospital

PICC line — Peripherally Inserted Central Catheter-a long, small slender tube usually inserted into one of the large veins in the arm and threaded into a large vein above the right side of the heart, used to give intravenous medicines or fluids or extract blood

Prosthesis — an artificial device to replace a missing part of the body

Wound vacuum, V.A.C. — Vacuum Assisted Closure, a device used to conduct negative pressure to a vacuum dressing to extract infectious materials, used to promote healing in acute or chronic wounds

Wound Care Center — a facility that specializes in care for patients with chronic wounds, often related to complications from vascular disorders, pressure sores, diabetes and traumatic wounds, outpatient center often on a hospital campus

Order Info.

To order a book for yourself, a friend, or family member,
visit www.SeveredYetWhole.com
or call 302.856.6649.
Also available from your favorite bookstore.

For autographed books,
to schedule speaking engagements,
to ask questions or post a comment,
contact Stephen and Betty
at

www.SeveredYetWhole.com

Bulk Discounts available through
Fruitbearer Publishing, LLC
P. O. Box 777, Georgetown, DE 19947
302.856.6649 • FAX 302.856.7742
info@fruitbearer.com
www.fruitbearer.com